INSPIRED BY

Endangered Species

Animals and Plants in Fabric Perspectives

Donna Marcinkowski DeSoto
Forewords by Kim O'Keefe Beck, PhD
and J. Drew Lanham, PhD

SCHIFFER
PUBLISHING

4880 Lower Valley Road • Atglen, PA 19310

Please find attached the signed Copyright Permission granting you permission to use information from the IUCN Red List in your book as described.

It is always very gratifying to hear stories of how the Red List is being used to inspire other people, particularly in creative ways by artists like yourself. I have realised in recent years that despite all the best science writing, the most effective way to communicate what is happening to the species on our planet to the wider public is through various forms of art. The quilts made by your artists are very beautiful and inspirational, so I wish you all success with your book.
Best wishes,

Craig Hilton-Taylor
Head Red List Unit
Global Species Programme, IUCN

OTHER SCHIFFER BOOKS BY THE AUTHOR:

Inspired by Elvis: Art Quilts Celebrating the King, foreword by Charles L. Hughes, ISBN 978-0-7643-5524-0

Inspired by the Beatles: An Art Quilt Challenge, ISBN 978-0-7643-4700-9

Inspired by the National Parks: Their Landscapes and Wildlife in Fabric Perspectives, ISBN 978-0-7643-5119-8

OTHER SCHIFFER BOOKS ON RELATED SUBJECTS:

Inside a Bald Eagle's Nest: A Photographic Journey through the American Bald Eagle Nesting Season, Teena Ruark Gorrow & Craig A. Koppie, ISBN 978-0-7643-4464-0

Contemporary Wildlife Art, Cindy Ann Coldiron, ISBN 978-0-7643-4864-8

Art Quilts International: Abstract & Geometric, Martha Sielman, ISBN 978-0-7643-5220-1

This book is derived from independent research by the author and artists. This book is not sponsored, endorsed, or otherwise affiliated with IUCN Red List, USFWS, Defenders of Wildlife, Wild Foundation, or any other groups, companies or organizations, or products mentioned herein, including Angelina, Bernina, Cherrywood Fabrics, DecoArt, Fabric Magic, Fabrico Markers, Gelli Plates, HandiQuilter, Innova Longarm, Lumiere paint, Lutradur, Micron pens, Neocolor, Pellon, Peltex, Pigma Pens, Puffy 3-D Paint, Seta Paints, Texture Magic, Tsukineko Inks, Ultrasuede, Wendy Richardson Hand-Dyes, Wonder-Under, and others.

Cover design by Brenda McCallum
Cover image: *Amur Leopard* by Ricki Selva
Title page image: Detail of *Cape Sable Seaside Sparrow* by Dottie Dane
Spine image: Detail of *Mandrill* by Eileen Thomas
Back cover image: *Loggerhead Turtle* by Karin Täuber
Type set in Sabon

ISBN: 978-0-7643-5789-3
Printed in China
Published by Schiffer Publishing, Ltd.
4880 Lower Valley Road
Atglen, PA 19310
Phone: (610) 593-1777; Fax: (610) 593-2002
E-mail: Info@schifferbooks.com
Web: www.schifferbooks.com

For our complete selection of fine books on this and related subjects, please visit our website at www.schifferbooks.com. You may also write for a free catalog.

Schiffer Publishing's titles are available at special discounts for bulk purchases for sales promotions or premiums. Special editions, including personalized covers, corporate imprints, and excerpts, can be created in large quantities for special needs. For more information, contact the publisher.

We are always looking for people to write books on new and related subjects. If you have an idea for a book, please contact us at proposals@schifferbooks.com.

To my children, Andy and Aimee DeSoto, to their generation, the next, and the next. These are the reasons we need to pay attention now and make the necessary changes to protect the precious animals and plants on our planet.

CONTENTS

Asiatic Lion

Channel-Billed Toucan

BIODIVERSITY AND THE FIRECROWN
by Peter Hodum
117

Giraffe

Hippopotamus

Honduran Emerald

WHAT ABOUT THE WETLANDS?
by John Overland
158

ON MAMMALS
AND REVIVING SPECIES
by Janet Rachlow and Jim Witham
252

ART AND HEART: OUR PLACE
IN THE STORY
by Vance Martin
262

Jaguar

Komodo Dragon

FOREWORD
Kim O'Keefe Beck, PhD

At its heart, conservation is a love story. A story born of love for wildlife and the wild lands they depend on. A story propelled by hope and sustained by the conviction that in working together, we can save species from extinction.

My particular story follows the path of a good many biologists of my generation. As a child, I was glued to the TV watching *Mutual of Omaha's Wild Kingdom*. A profound love of wildness was instilled in me by the freedom to prowl the Sonoran Desert surrounding my home in Tucson, Arizona. Days were spent rehabbing kangaroo rats, catching "Horny Toads" (a.k.a. horned lizards), chasing quail, watching zany roadrunners zip across the desert with snakes dangling from their beaks, constructing habitats for desert tortoises, and lying awake in my bed waiting to hear the yip-howls of coyotes in the night. When we moved to Oregon, forest-dwelling wildlife, including the hilarious antics of western gray squirrels, fulfilled my longing to observe and be immersed in nature. A child of the '70s, I grew up in a United States essentially devoid of gray wolves. Reading *Never Cry Wolf* by Farley Mowat when I was ten years old led me to understand that this was by design: a centuries-long extermination campaign nearly eradicated gray wolves from the continental United States by the 1950s. I was enraged and disheartened; a keystone species was missing from the ecosystems throughout most of our country, and the leaders of previous generations had sanctioned its loss. So when, years later, I encountered wild wolves while hiking to one of my research sites, as the result of the successful 1995 wolf reintroduction program, it took my breath away. I had just crossed a creek, and as I came up over the rise I saw and heard a wolf up and to my right on a rocky outcrop. Another wolf, very dark gray, was skirting the edge of the forest ahead. After years of mourning their loss, seeing them wild in their natural environment was beyond

thrilling. I was deeply moved and felt a profound sense of joy and hope. Conservation works.

My days are no longer spent researching how climate influences small populations in the Greater Yellowstone Ecosystem. However, I now have the great honor of working to protect endangered species and the Endangered Species Act that protects them, as a member of the Board of Trustees for Defenders of Wildlife. This group was instrumental in the reintroduction of those wolves to Yellowstone so many years ago. While my encounter with wolves was a pivotal experience and solidified my commitment to conduct research that could inform important decision making for conserving biodiversity, it also served to highlight the truth that knowledge alone won't save species. Just as wolves were nearly eradicated, then protected and reintroduced, and are again hunted in some states, values and perceptions change. Habitat availability, quality, connectivity, and climate are changing. Species are becoming extinct at unprecedented rates: dozens every day. In the US alone, 1,276 species are listed as endangered and many more are severely threatened. Some might ask, with so many important issues facing society today, why care about this? I believe the answer is simple and compelling. First, extinction is forever. Second, an ecosystem destroyed by development or drilling will never again provide the services such as clean air, water, biodiversity, food, and medicines that we require for sustained healthy life on this planet. Finally, and perhaps most importantly, who are we to deny future generations the wonder of wildlife and wild places? Wildness matters. It feeds our souls, nourishes our connection to place and time, and inspires our imagination. So, for me, protecting wildness, for the sake of wildness alone, is enough. I want to leave my children a world where they can still know for themselves how it feels to be in a wild space with wild creatures. To know that we are a part of something vast, complex, and beautiful. To be humbled by and exult in this beautiful world of ours. The challenge is daunting. But the imperative is clear. And the lesson of the wolves in Yellowstone remains: if people care enough, conservation works.

As a biologist, I have ascribed to the philosophy so well stated in a quote by Baba Dioum, "In the end we will conserve only what we love, we will love only what we understand, and we will understand only what we are taught." While science matters and is an essential component of conserving endangered species, when it comes to inspiring people to action, my thoughts have shifted. I'd alter his last sentence to "we will understand only what we experience." It is here that science leaves off and art moves to the fore.

Throughout the ages, artists and their work have played a vital role in conservation by helping us experience our connection with the natural world and with the other inhabitants with whom we share this one glorious Earth. Rachel Carson once said, "It is not half so important to know as to feel." Art allows us to *feel* our connection.

As I set my eyes upon these extraordinary quilts, the words of Jane Goodall resonate. "What you do makes a difference. And you have to decide what difference you want to make." It is as powerful and simple as that. With every stitch in these inspiring works of art, these artists have sewn a connection among themselves, us, and the imperiled species they hope to save from extinction. In so doing, they are making a difference. I give them my thanks. Here's hoping that their vision and artistry inspires us all. We all play a role. It's up to each of us to decide what it is.

Your conservation story might mean writing your representatives to support and uphold the Endangered Species Act, or supporting a conservation organization, or volunteering for habitat restoration. Or it might mean simply exploring the outdoors with your children, or visiting national parks and wildlife refuges, or refusing the straw and reducing your use of plastic to protect marine species; it might mean recycling, planting native or pollinator-friendly plants in your garden, or taking your own reusable coffee mug, water bottle, and grocery bags with you. Or it might mean creating your own art. Whatever you choose, your choice matters. You, too, can make a meaningful difference.

Kim O'Keefe Beck, PhD
Biologist, Defenders of Wildlife Board of Directors member

June 16, 2018

Staghorn Coral

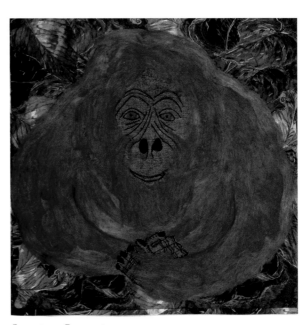

Sumatran Orangutan

FOREWORD

J. Drew Lanham, PhD

Endangered. Endangered is the last gasp before extinction and reality's final frontier. As a conservation ecologist, I've spent decades perched anxiously on the rim of the grim reality that is forever gone. As a child I watched a memorable episode of the *ABC Afterschool Special*. It featured a cartoon that was an adaptation of Fred Bodsworth's classic children's book, *Last of the Curlews*. It was about the dwindling of a species, the Eskimo curlew, down to one last lonely bird. I was pulled into an animated world of wondrous avian migration and thoughtless human exploitation that personalized the struggle for survival in a way that stuck deep down inside me. That cartoon so entranced me that I began to read everything I could about other dwindling wild things.

Encyclopedias and tomes borrowed from libraries opened up the door to a world of all-consuming wildness. Although birds were my first love, I found finned, furred, scaled, and slimy-skinned things fascinating, too. I was obsessed with discovering as much as I could in the glorious splendor of photographs in print. On the television show *Mutual of Omaha's Wild Kingdom*, Marlin Perkins and Jim Fowler introduced me to the idea of conservation as they traveled the world. I made it known to family and friends that maybe one day I'd be like Jim, an intrepid adventurer saving wildlife: a conservationist.

For all of the imagining I did as a boy, my dreams of saving wildlife became a reality. It is my daily work. The endangered list has sadly expanded to some 1,200 vertebrate species. The habitats they depend on are often equally imperiled, fragmented into bits and pieces; scraps of wetlands, forests, and grasslands besieged by development and climate change. The oceans holding many endangered species are also imperiled. Pollution and overfishing carry much of the blame. Both for terrestrial and aquatic habitats, the wild card in the conservation quilt is climate change.

In this wonderful volume of artful homage to conservation, we get to marvel over the dedication of skilled craftspeople who've given time and talent to some of our most precious and imperiled wild beings, including the Eskimo curlew. The artistry on display in these pages will perhaps create a new sense of urgency. I define wildlife conservation as an intense caring for some wild being that leads one to fight for it beyond the edge. Thumb through the pages of this treasury. Linger on the forms and faces of species you know and those you don't. Try to feel the textures of warty toad skin, soft cat fur, and hardened ferret fang. Flock and fly with the feather beings you find. Immerse mind and heart in what remains and perhaps the work here will move you to work for reversing extinction's savage trends. It is my hope that you will find some feeling in each and every stitch and piece that come together here.

J. Drew Lanham
Alumni distinguished professor of wildlife ecology and master teacher, Clemson University

Audubon Society Board of Directors member
Author, *The Home Place: Memoirs of a Colored Man's Love Affair with Nature*

May 16, 2018

ACKNOWLEDGMENTS

Heartfelt love and appreciation goes to—

Kurt, for logical suggestions, editorial advice, and especially for technical expertise the morning he "found" this manuscript, which I was convinced had fallen into a bottomless black hole and was not endangered, but extinct. Also for providing me the means to a wonderful life where I am able to pursue causes, passions, interests, and other distractions.

Andy and Aimee, for all manner of help, support, and encouragement from day one.

Nancy and Bill Adams, for their grace, for their courage, for the reminders that all will be well, and for their unparalleled example of love.

Sandra Korinchak, the best editor ever, Pete Schiffer, Carey Massimini, Peggy Kellar, and all of the creative minds at Schiffer Publishing for providing me opportunity for a forum and making another dream happen.

Kim O'Keefe Beck, Jim Fowler, Peter Hodum, Drew Lanham, Vance Martin, John Overland, Janet Rachlow, and Jim Witham: these scientists, professors, and conservationists cared so much about the topic of this book that they shared invaluable perspectives and insight. Wendy Strahm provided a unique narrative and also gave vital guidance.

This fine community of quilt artists who did significant work, and for their camaraderie and support. Also to the numerous talented photographers who granted permission to use their work for reference and inspiration.

Mars Imgrund, for research assistance, and Joyce Carrier and Becky Koenig, for editorial help and advice.

Beth Shafer and Norma Fredrickson, for their loyal and tireless friendship.

Jeanne Coglianese, Dottie Dane, Kerry Faraone, Carrie Fowler, Kay Fowler, Roddy Gabel, Barbara and Tom Kauffman, Linda and Craig Moore, Carole Nicholas, Starla Phelps, Luana Rubin, Susan Sladek, Marianne Stana, and Jennifer Weilbach, for helping hands along the way.

To my brother Frank, who came up with the idea of an endangered species project.

To the IUCN, from which most of the research herein was derived, and to everyone who gives a hoot about conservation.

To God, who is the only one who really knows how all of this will play out.

And last but not least, to Quinn Wolfson, pictured below: a rare breed, who provided precious relief on an as-needed basis (and it was needed often). This little girl serves as a reminder to me of the wonder and miracle of life.

Photo by Jason Wolfson

INTRODUCTION

Admittedly, I was one of those people who released a balloon into the air at a funeral, considered hiring a company to get rid of the mosquitoes in my yard, regularly forgot my reusable grocery shopping bags in the car, and let the water run in the sink while brushing my teeth. What harm can be done to this big, wild world by just me? But when you add together these and many other oversights, not just mine, but everyone else's, *much* harm is being done.

The highlight of our last vacation was a sunrise stroll on the beach that went from casual shell collecting to experiencing the rescue of a nest of hawksbill turtle eggs by the Emerald Isle Sea Turtle Patrol. What I had thought were huge tire tracks leading to the sea turned out to be something entirely different. As we watched the volunteers follow the turtle tracks to locate a nest, dig, and document and relocate 63 eggs, I marveled at their patience with passersby. They answered every single question asked by the group that had gathered with vast knowledge and detail, all the while focusing utmost care on the squishy ping-pong ball eggs: reburying them farther up toward the dunes, where they would be safer, covering the top of the area with sand and then mesh wire to protect them from predators. It was fascinating, my first time witnessing this loving act of humans to rescue a species in peril, and I couldn't get the experience out of my mind. When you think about it, aren't we all endangered? On the long drive home came the idea . . . in lieu of flowers. I said it out loud, and my husband said, "What?" Someday, tell the people that in lieu of flowers they can give money to the Emerald Isle Sea Turtle Patrol. I would really like that.

My mission to learn as much as I can about endangered species was born. I love to write, I love to quilt, and I love quilters and know a lot of them. That is how this book came to be.

When I announced the topic of this project in the quilter network, there were a few guidelines and parameters, but the most important thing I asked everyone to do before they put thread to fabric was to thoroughly research their subject. It

Classification of Living Organisms

seemed to me that the more artists learned about their species, the stronger the quilts would be. Much research was based on the information presented online by the IUCN Red List. The purposes of the Red List are to provide scientifically based information on the status of species and subspecies at a global level, to draw attention to the magnitude and importance of threatened biodiversity, to influence national and international policymaking and decision making, and to share information to guide actions to conserve biological diversity.

An interesting thing happened while the quilts were being made. Whenever the artists got together and talked about their quilts, it sounded like a gathering of scientists.

An interesting thing happened when we photographed the quilts at Schiffer Publishing. The staff there who came into the photo studio to see the quilts kept remarking, "I didn't know *that* species is endangered!"

Education can be transformative in unexpected ways: causing us to pay attention, ask more questions, and even to care more, or differently.

It is important to mention that people think of different meanings when they hear the word "endangered." There are also varying degrees of endangered-ness. This book contains a wide range of endangeredness, from species that are alarmingly close to extinction to those species that are at risk, but to a lesser severity. Because I am a hopeful person, and I believe there are measures we can take to improve the outcomes of endangered species, toward the end of this book are four "success stories." These are examples of species whose situations, while still of concern, are improving, and their populations are successfully reviving.

Regarding particular designations, in an article on Britannica.com by Holly Dublin, she states: "The need for separate definitions of 'endangered' and 'threatened' species resulted in the development of various categorization systems, each containing definitions and criteria by which a species can be classified according to its risk of extinction." For specific information, take a look at these criteria as labeled by the IUCN and other organizations mentioned in the following pages.

In this book, 182 at-risk species appear in alphabetical order by their common name. As you read the narratives by conservation experts, sprinkled throughout, and view images of the quilts, there is an opportunity to learn something about the species depicted. Each listing contains the Latin name, the phylum and class for animals, and the kingdom and family for plants, the designation and status of the species, a brief description, where the species is located, what the main threats are, and some of the conservation steps that are being taken, or could be taken, to try to save the species.

The information here is not comprehensive, and because of the nature of this subject there is constant flux. We hear news of endangered species every day. In fact, the day this manuscript was completed, three pertinent events happened. A newborn baby of one of the golden lion tamarins at the National Zoo in Washington, DC, accidentally fell off the back of one of its parents and died. The state of Hawaii approved a bill banning the sale of sunscreen containing chemicals believed to be harmful to coral reefs and other ocean life surrounding the islands. And an outcry occurred over a controversy where a woman killed a giraffe in South Africa. Some species, by the time this manuscript goes to print, may be extinct. Others may have moved up or down on the chart below depicting endangeredness categories. Numbers rise and fall, statuses change, but make no mistake, general trends are species in decline, and the alarm is sounding.

Conservation Status Classification Codes

The International Union for Conservation of Nature (IUCN) and NatureServe have developed categories to indicate the conservation status of species and the risk of extinction. The categories are similar, but use different terminology. Moreover, these organizations have developed separate critera and methods to determine how to evaluate and classify the conservation status and risk of extinction. The graphic below is provided to identify the categories and the terms used by both organizations. For more information about these categories, visit www.iucnredlist.org and www.natureserve.org.

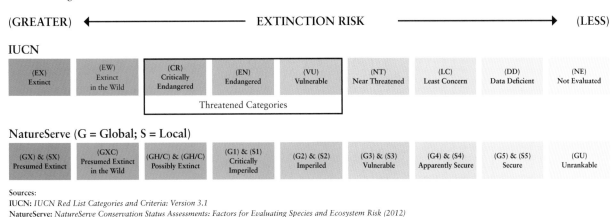

Sources:
IUCN: *IUCN Red List Categories and Criteria: Version 3.1*
NatureServe: *NatureServe Conservation Status Assessments: Factors for Evaluating Species and Ecosystem Risk (2012)*

CONSERVATION AND THE IUCN
Wendy Strahm

Nothing can be as satisfying as seeing a species on the road to extinction and then watching it come back. Or as depressing as seeing a species disappear forever, during our lifetime, and knowing that this should not be happening on our watch. Sadly the decline in biodiversity is a fact, and each decade, as world population grows, we continue to edge out species that we share this planet with. I hope that as people understand what we are doing to nature, each and every person will work together to reverse the trend and ensure that future generations will be able to enjoy the myriad of species that our generation has been blessed with.

My journey in nature conservation started as a child, when I was fascinated by species of everything. I started collections of rocks, shells, feathers, fossils, plants, and skulls; in fact, anything my mother allowed in my room. My family moved to Greece, where I discovered the Mediterranean and had a great biology teacher who convinced me to become a biologist. I studied biology and geology at Oberlin College and was most influenced by going on "Sunday walks" with a wonderful old retired botanist, Dr. George Jones. This was at a time when everyone said he was a dying breed; someone who knew all the plants around him and loved sharing this knowledge with students, when "real" biology was changing from observing the natural world to putting species into blenders to extract their DNA.

I was fortunate to have the opportunity to join a project in the Indian Ocean island of Mauritius, working with some of the rarest birds and plants in the world. These species were on the verge of extinction, but nobody was too worried about them, particularly the plants. While working there, I met some conservation legends such as Don Merton of New Zealand, who saved the black robin and kakapo (an extraordinary nocturnal, flightless parrot pictured in a quilt on page 120) from extinction, and Tom Cade from the US, the architect of one of the great conservation success stories, which was the restoration of the peregrine falcon to the East Coast of the US. These people were an inspiration and taught me to never give up hope, even when a species was down to its last few individuals. Our work in saving the Mauritius kestrel, pink pigeon, and echo parakeet, all down to just a few pairs, as well as some plants such as the "café marron" ("wild coffee") of Rodrigues, which was down to a single individual, was proof that it is never too late.

Twelve years later, I moved back to Switzerland to work as the IUCN plants officer, and suddenly rather than just worrying about the plants on some islands in the Indian Ocean, there was the whole world to be concerned with. There are many plants facing extinction. IUCN manages the IUCN Red List, a global, collaborative effort to identify all threatened species of plants and animals. A globally threatened species is defined as one with a high risk of extinction, using a number of criteria, and the species at highest risk are designated as "Critically Endangered" (CR), "Endangered" (EN), and "Vulnerable" (VU). Most of the species portrayed in these quilts are on the IUCN Red List, but not all of them, since the IUCN Red List includes only species that are threatened with extinction at a global level. However, there are many more species that are disappearing at a local level: they are threatened or extinct in one place when they may still be relatively common somewhere else. Given the gradual reduction in biodiversity throughout the world, any loss or reduction of a population in one place is cause for great concern, and the saying "think globally, act locally" has never been more important. Only by people taking care of the biodiversity in the areas where they live will we be able to stem the tide of global extinctions.

Saving species requires saving the habitat in which they occur and combating the drivers that are causing their disappearance, whether it is through habitat destruction, invasive species that overtake

Red Panda

Tiger

the place of the species that should naturally be found in the area, unsustainable use, or the rapid change in climate caused by a growing human population using increasing amounts of fossil fuels. Protected areas play a big role in conserving wildlife (see *Inspired by the National Parks*), but these areas need to be managed well in order to provide a safe haven for biodiversity. Species need to be conserved outside protected areas. It is here that everyone has an individual responsibility. As you view the species in these marvelous works of art, contemplate what small changes we can make in our lifestyles that will reduce the pressure on the natural world we all share. Whether it is by reducing our travel by car or airplane, eating less meat, using less plastic, putting up nest boxes and insect hotels, helping frogs cross the road at spawning time, or a myriad of other activities, we can all do our bit.

Wendy Strahm
former IUCN plants officer, Switzerland

April 4, 2018

Wendy is currently working on a project to restore ospreys as a breeding species in Switzerland, which she says is going well. See www.ospreys.ch

LIST OF ACRONYMS

CITES: Convention on International Trade in Endangered Species of Wild Flora and Fauna

ESA: Ecological Society of America

IUCN: International Union for Conservation of Nature and Natural Resources

NMFS: National Marine Fisheries Service

NPS: National Park Service

USDA: US Department of Agriculture

USFWS: US Fish & Wildlife Service

WWF: World Wildlife Fund

ACALYPHA WIGGINSII

Cathron Birge, Fredericksburg, Virginia

- *Acalypha wigginsii*
- Plantae/Euphorbiaceae family
- Not evaluated by the IUCN Red List, regionally listed as Critically Endangered in the Galápagos
- This unusual looking plant, a scraggly woody herb, has drooping red flowers that resemble chenille.
- Located on Santa Cruz Island, in the Galápagos

- In peril due to human interaction: trampling and construction. Installation of telecommunications antennae has disturbed and destroyed populations.
- Close monitoring unexpectedly revealed a rise in numbers of these plants. Installation of fences may provide protection. Periodic weeding of the areas where they are found has enhanced colonizing, leading to new plans aiding long-term survival.

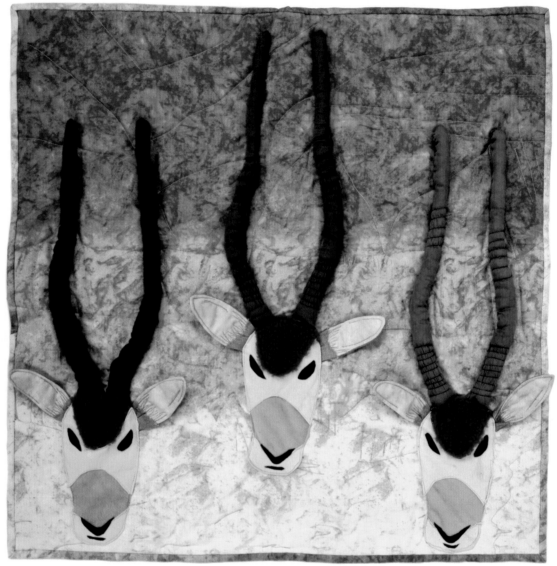

Tina Lewis, Parker, Colorado

- *Addax nasomaculatus*
- Chordata/Mammalia
- Critically Endangered: population trend decreasing
- This animal weighs between 220 to 300 pounds and is 37 to 45 inches tall to the shoulder. Its most noticeable characteristic is its 30-to-43-inch-long twisted horns. The coat color changes depending on the season, from gray brown to white. Because of its short legs and chunky build, this antelope is slow moving. They travel in herds of five to 20, and they eat grass and leaves. They are nicely adapted to desert life; in the heat of the day, they rest, and they feed at night and early in the day.
- They live in the Sahara Desert in Niger and Chad in Africa.
- They are in danger because they are preyed upon by cheetahs, leopards, lions, and African wild dogs. They are also poached. The oil industry is making their habitat unsatisfactory.
- To recover the species, IUCN suggests support for established reserves in Africa, new protected areas, and incentives for locals to protect wildlife. Perhaps hunting ought to be disallowed and better regulated. Captive breeding programs leading to reintroduction might then be successful.

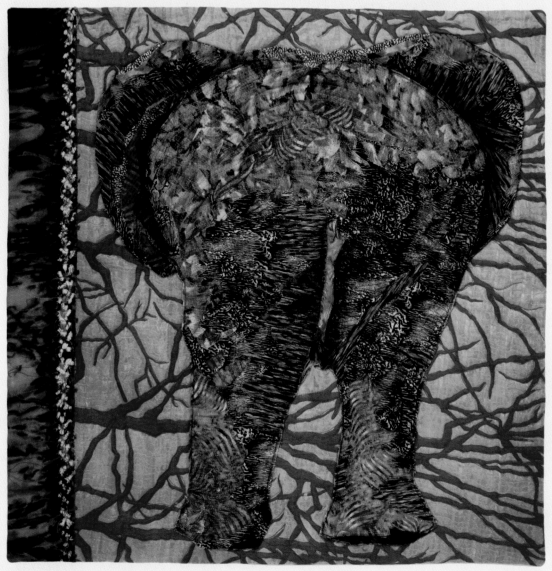

Barbara Hollinger, Vienna, Virginia

- *Loxodonta africana*
- Chordata/Mammalia
- Vulnerable: population increasing
- African elephants are a keystone species. National Geographic says these are organisms that help define a whole ecosystem; without them, the ecosystem would be dramatically different, or it could even cease to exist. These elephants are the largest land mammals on Earth. They are highly intelligent and live in family groups. Herds roam and forage through tropical and open woodlands, savannas, scrub, and deserts.
- Exist in 36 countries in sub-Saharan Africa

- They are at risk due to loss of habitat and trophy hunting. Wide-scale poaching has greatly reduced the population. Their tusks are highly prized especially in China, where they are carved into decorative items for sale and trade.
- Conservation plans include protection of habitat, and prosecution of poachers and traders in ivory. A full ban on trophy hunting would protect the remaining herds. In addition to providing wildlife sanctuaries, effective management is needed in agricultural areas where herds can cause damage to crops and villages.

Laura Catherine Gilmartin, Stafford, Virginia

- *Panthera leo*
- Chordata/Mammalia
- Vulnerable: population decreasing
- This animal, golden brown in color, is easily recognized by the long mane encircling the head. They have no natural predators, are 4.5 to 6.5 feet tall, and weigh 265 to 420 pounds. They are territorial and prey upon large mammals, including zebras, wildebeest, and antelopes. The groups they live in are called prides.
- Located in western and central Africa in savannas and deserts
- In danger as a result of trophy hunting, illegal bush meat industry, and widespread killing by people to protect livestock. Their habitat is also diminishing.
- Better government regulation and oversight of trophy hunting and bush meat industry is needed. Conservation programs in place must be managed and governed better to prevent illegal killings.

Teresa Bristow, Springfield, Virginia

- *Lycaon pictus* (also commonly called the painted hunting dog)
- Chordata/Mammalia
- Endangered: population trend decreasing
- Wild dogs can reach a height of 30 to 40 inches and weigh from 40 to 70 pounds. They have long legs, large rounded ears, and a unique patchy-colored coat. They have four toes on each foot. Packs have strong family bonds, and fighting among the pack is rare. Wild dogs communicate at a high level, using expansive auditory language and visual cues involving ears, tail, mouth, and back position. These are hunting dogs, and their preferred prey is mainly medium-sized antelope. The average litter size is ten pups, and they typically live for eight years.
- They are found mostly in southern Africa in grassy plains, semideserts, and savannas.
- Many factors are leading to the decimation of the wild dogs, but the largest are humans and loss of habitat. Dogs fall victim to ranchers or farmers who mistakenly regard them as a threat to their livestock. Once this is perceived, the misunderstood animals are shot or poisoned. Others are run over by cars. As the human population grows, the natural habitat of wild dogs shrinks. East Africa has a myriad of infectious diseases such as rabies and parvo that affect the population. These dogs hunt as a pack over a large range, and the loss of any member has consequences for the rest. Lions and hyenas steal hard-earned prey of wild dogs, and lions kill dogs if an opportunity arises.
- The Painted Dog Protection Initiative is attempting to reduce the loss of dogs by using antisnare and reflective collars, and by spreading the word to increase awareness of their plight. The Painted Dog Conservation team monitors the activity of its packs by using radio collars and heading antipoaching efforts. A rehabilitation facility focuses on the safe recovery of injured dogs, which can then be returned to their pack or reintroduced to the wild.

ALEUTIAN SHIELD FERN

Nancy B. Adams, Annandale, Virginia

- *Polystichum aleuticum*
- Plantae/Dryopteridaceae family
- Endangered, according to USFWS
- Fern, 6.5 inches tall, with tooth-edged leaflets on fronds
- Endemic to Adak Island, Alaska

- Because they grow in moist crevices and along rock walls at approximately 1,100-foot elevation, rockslides caused by frequent earthquakes and volcanic eruptions pose danger. Other threats include caribou and invasive Norway rats.
- Conservation ideas: keep caribou away, restrict public access. Cultivation efforts have failed thus far.

AMUR LEOPARD

Ricki Selva, Fort Myer, Virginia

- *Panthera pardus orientalis*
- Chordata/Mammalia
- Vulnerable: population decreasing; WWF classifies them as Critically Endangered.
- One of nine subspecies of leopards, this is the rarest of the world's biggest cats, weighing between 55 to 105 pounds. Adapted for life in a harsh winter climate, this cat's fur is only about an inch long in the summer but triples in length and becomes lighter in color with the arrival of winter. The pale color of fur helps camouflage them in the snow. Their legs are longer than other leopards, enabling them to walk easily through the snow. Secretive, solitary, and nocturnal, one leopard can occupy territory as vast as 60 square miles. Their diet includes hares, wild boar, deer, and moose.
- Found mainly in temperate and coniferous forests between the Amur River in Russia and northeast China

- Main threats are habitat loss and fragmentation through development, logging, forest fires, and climate change. Illegal killing for wildlife trade and as retaliation due to conflict with humans, as well as prey depletion by poaching of deer and wild boar, are taking a toll. Because of inbreeding, they are vulnerable to disease and genetic abnormalities.
- Aggressive enforcement to prevent poaching, transboundary protection, research, advocacy, increased monitoring, and education are necessary to preserve the species. A coalition of 15 international and Russian nongovernmental organizations (NGOs) have pooled their resources to help create ALTA (Amur Leopard and Tiger Alliance).

ANDEAN FLAMINGO

Sharon Burke Rixmann, Manassas, Virginia

- *Phoenicoparrus andinus*
- Chordata/Aves
- Vulnerable: population trend stable
- This social bird has pale pink and white feathers on the upper body, with darker pink on the neck and lower body. It has black flight and tail feathers and is the only flamingo with yellow legs. The average weight is almost 9 pounds, and they are approximately 3.5 feet tall. Algae are their primary food source, and their beaks contain special filtration abilities. They can travel hundreds of miles a day in search of food.

- Located in Peru, Argentina, and Chile
- At risk because of habitat disturbances caused by mining, water pollution, and construction. Eggs are poached by natives.
- The Flamingo Specialist Group is actively publicizing the vulnerability of the remaining Andean flamingos in order to educate the public about environmental threats.

Karen Johnston, Fallbrook, California

- *Anaxyrus californicus*
- Chordata/Amphibia
- Endangered: population trend decreasing
- This is a small toad, up to 3 inches long. They live in creeks and other natural drainage areas, and their preferred diet is the velvet tree ant. Do you know the differences between a toad and a frog? Generally, because there are a few exceptions, toads have shorter legs and unwebbed feet, and their skin is rough. Frogs have smooth skin and webbed feet, live closer to water, and jump higher. Either can have warts.

- Located from Southern California to Baja California, and in Mexico
- Development is causing habitat destruction, and they suffer predation by nonnative species such as bullfrogs.
- Determine specific areas where they live to avoid development and recreation. Manage nonnative predators.

Cheryl Deene Hurd, Washington, DC

Asiatic Black Bear

- *Ursus thibetanus* (also known as the Himalayan black bear)
- Chordata/Mammalia
- Vulnerable: population decreasing
- These bears have a black coat of fur and a distinctive white, V-shaped marking on the chest.
- Located in regions in central and southern Asia, from Afghanistan to Japan, and south to Thailand. There is a small population found as far north as Russia.
- For 3,000 years people have hunted these bears, mainly for their paws and gall bladders; their dried bile is used in traditional Chinese medicines and is believed to contain numerous healing properties.
- Despite the hunting ban throughout their natural range (except for Japan, where numbers are considered to be increasing), these bears remain heavily threatened both by hunting and habitat loss. In addition, they are captured as pets, for sport, or to spend the rest of their days in the misery of bile farms.

Laura Catherine Gilmartin, Stafford, Virginia

ASIATIC LION

- *Panthera leo* subsp. *persica*
- Chordata/Mammalia
- Endangered: population trend increasing
- These lions have a short, sparse mane. One way to distinguish them from other lions is that they have a long fold of skin running along their underside. They grow to nearly 10 feet in length and weigh 250 to 400 pounds. Their life span is 18 to 20 years. They consume deer, antelope, bear, and cattle.
- There is a population isolated in Gujarat, India.
- The species is in trouble because they were hunted to near extinction. More threats include vulnerability to disease, poaching, human encroachment for farming and urbanization, and natural disasters, such as fires.
- To save this species, the Asiatic Lion Reintroduction Project is introducing a second independent population at another site at an Indian wildlife sanctuary. Locals are not enthusiastic about this project. Various organizations are attempting to safeguard remaining lions. Threats need to be further identified and actively monitored.

Jeanne Coglianese, Haymarket, Virginia

Atlantic Bluefin Tuna

- *Thunnus thynnus*
- Chordata/Actinopterygii
- Endangered: population trend decreasing
- This is one of the fastest and largest fish in the world. These warm-blooded fish average 550 pounds and are 6.5 feet in length. They live for approximately 15 years. Their metallic coloring helps camouflage them from above and below in the water.
- These fish are in the waters off Newfoundland and Iceland, down to the Gulf of Mexico, and in the Mediterranean Sea.
- Tuna are becoming extinct because they are a valuable source for sushi. One single fish has been sold for 1.75 million dollars. Such high prices make them a prized catch.
- Best conservation efforts would be better enforcement and control of illegal fishing.

ATLANTIC STURGEON

Priscilla B. Godfrey, Philomont, Virginia

- *Acipenser sturio*
- Chordata/Actinopterygii
- Critically Endangered: population decreasing
- This fish is bluish black or olive brown in color, is up to 14 feet long, and can weigh 80 pounds. It lives in salt water but hatches and spawns in fresh water; the life span is 60 years.
- They live in rivers from Maine to Florida.
- They are in peril due to poor water quality, vessel strikes, and unintended catches, and their spawning areas are being dammed or dredged.
- Measures to revive the species include a fishery management plan, a moratorium on harvesting, preservation to focus on improved habitat, designing fishing nets that do not catch the sturgeon, requiring that Fish and Wildlife be notified about dams and dredging of spawning areas, and reduction of pollutants in waterways.

Shannon Dart, Springfield, Virginia

- *Zaglossus attenboroughi*
- Chordata/Mammalia
- Critically Endangered: population trend decreasing
- This nocturnal creature has short, dense fur, raw umber in color. Spines are on the back, and when it is afraid, it can roll itself up into a ball, much like a hedgehog. Weighing 11 to 22 pounds, these antisocial animals mate once a year in July. Do you know what a baby echidna is called? A puggle. The female has a pouch where she keeps her babies after they hatch. These animals have no teeth, but their tongue is covered in spines. The long "beak" is used to probe into the mud to forage for food.

- Lives on the mountain forest floor at Cyclops Mountain in Papua New Guinea
- Their livelihood is precarious due to hunting and habitat loss.
- To revive the species, conservationists are working with local communities to raise awareness and to enforce the protection of the Cyclops Mountains Strict Nature Reserve. More research and monitoring is needed.

BACTRIAN CAMEL

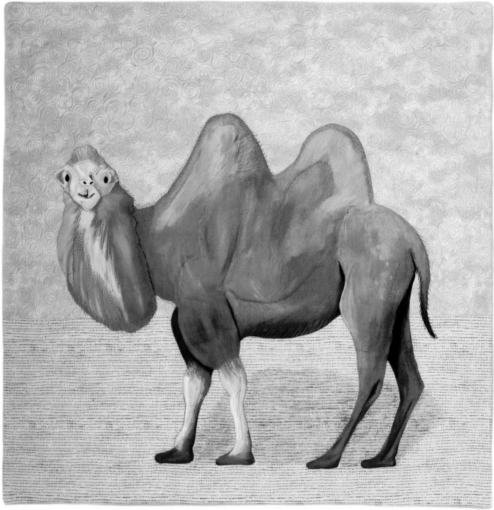

Barbara Polston, Phoenix, Arizona

- *Camelus ferus*
- Chordata/Mammalia
- Critically Endangered: population decreasing
- These animals stand over 7 feet tall and can weigh up to 1,800 pounds. They live an average of 30 years, graze mostly on grass, and have four separate stomachs. Their dark-brown or dirty-gray fur, 10 inches long, keeps them warm when temperatures are –20°F. When temperatures rise in the desert to over 100°F, they shed their coat. Two rows of eyelashes protect their eyes from wind and sand and harsh conditions in the desert. They have the ability to close their nostrils. This species has two humps that store fat. This gives them the ability to go for long periods without water; camels can live for a couple of weeks without food or drink when they are well nourished. When they have not had food or drink for a long time, the humps sag sideways and get smaller. A thirsty camel can drink 30 gallons of water in just 13 minutes. Camels are social and nonterritorial. Females have an average of 12 offspring in their lifetime. Humans have used camels for centuries as modes of transportation.
- They live in the Gobi Desert of Mongolia and China.
- Domesticated animals in the area have created competition for food. Humans hunt camels for meat, hides, wool, sinew, and bone. Leopards and wolves are their predators.
- A protected reserve has been created in an effort to revive the population in the wild. However, the reserve has been encroached upon by mining operations, and severe drought has caused considerable damage.

BAKER'S LARKSPUR

Sandi Goldman, Annandale, Virginia

- *Delphinium bakeri*
- Plantae/Ranunculaceae family
- Not evaluated by IUCN but listed as Endangered by the ESA
- A perennial herb that grows up to 26 inches tall. Flowers bloom from April through May, are purplish blue in color, and are pollinated by bees and hummingbirds.
- Endemic to California, found in Marin and Sonoma Counties

- Danger of extinction due to landslides, fires, consumption by invertebrates, trampling, roadside mowing, and damage from road crews. Farmers spray them because they are poisonous to livestock. Because of urban development, the population is small and the range is significantly restricted.
- Efforts to conserve the species include prohibition from killing or taking the plants, as directed by the California Endangered Species Act. Three new sites have been introduced to grow more.

Vanessa McCallum, Murfreesboro, Tennessee

BLACK RHINOCEROS

- *Diceros bicornis*
- Chordata/Mammalia
- Critically Endangered: population increasing
- Adults weigh 1,760 to 3,090 pounds and are 55 to 71 inches tall to their shoulders. They measure from 10 to just over 12 feet in length. They are herbivores (they eat only plants) and have a pointed lip, enabling them to eat fruit and leaves from trees and bushes. They are brown or gray with two horns, the longer of which can be 20 to 55 inches long. The horns are used for defense and digging for food. Black rhinos are solitary and have thick skin, fed upon by parasites. They are very aggressive and, despite their size, can run more than 30 miles per hour. Their life span is 35 to 50 years.
- They are found in savannas, grasslands, and deserts in southern and eastern Africa.
- Poachers kill them for their horns. Other large species such as elephants are threats, as well as habitat change, civil disturbances in the area (war), and ingestion of too much iron, causing health problems.
- Wildlife preserves breed and protect these animals. New laws are being passed to prevent the sale of rhino horns.

Sandy Kretzer, Burke, Virginia

BLACK-CAPPED VIREO

- *Vireo atricapilla*
- Chordata/Aves
- Vulnerable: population decreasing
- This small songbird is 4.5 inches long, with olive-green plumage and a bright white belly. Only the male has a black head. They eat insects and some varieties of berries, and they require scrubby deciduous thickets for nesting.
- They can be found in Oklahoma, Texas, and Mexico.
- Cowbirds lay eggs in vireo nests, and the cowbird chicks hatch first, dominating the food supply. This puts the population of vireo in a vulnerable state. Grazing livestock prevents tree growth, which damages the habitat.
- Cowbird removal efforts are attributed to local population increases. Prescribed burns allow growth of scrub oak habitat.

Barbara E. Kauffman, Waterford, Virginia

BLACK-FOOTED FERRET

- *Mustela nigripes*
- Chordata/Mammalia
- Endangered: population decreasing
- Species of carnivorous weasel that preys primarily on prairie dogs. They have a pale-tan body with black legs, feet, and tail tip, and a black mask is across the face and eyes. They are nocturnal and mostly solitary, except when females are raising their young.
- They live in prairies and grasslands and are native from Saskatchewan, Canada, to northern Chihuahua, Mexico.
- Their decline is mostly due to prairie dog eradication programs and sylvatic plague. They are also susceptible to canine distemper. The conversion of grassland to agricultural use affects the species negatively. Loss of genetic diversity through captive breeding of an initially small population harms their viability.
- Primary steps that can be taken include the continuation of a successful captive-breeding program under the guidance and management of a USFWS recovery program. In 1987 this species was considered the rarest mammal on Earth. This species was twice declared extinct in the past 50 years, but twice, tiny relict populations were discovered and monitored by scientists. A captive breeding program begun in 1985 by the Wyoming Game and Fish Department, in cooperation with the USFWS, from the last 18 individuals known in the wild, has brought this species back from the brink of extinction. Full recovery will require hard work among private landowners, non-profit organizations, Native American tribes, zoos, and state and federal agencies in the US, Canada, and Mexico. Habitats need to be preserved, restored, and managed. Invasive species disease needs to be controlled. Educate the public. Continue coordination and cooperation between public and private land and natural resources managers with an adequate funding commitment.

Karin Täuber, Blacksburg, Virginia

Blackburn's Sphinx Moth

- *Manduca blackburni*
- Arthropoda/Insecta
- Not evaluated by the IUCN Red List but designated Endangered by the ESA. This was the very first Hawaiian insect to be listed as an endangered species by the USFWS.
- This is Hawaii's largest insect, and it has a wingspan of up to 5 inches. Its wings are long and narrow, and the thick body tapers at each end. They are grayish brown with black markings towards the top, and five orange spots on either side of the abdomen. Larvae feed on native aiea trees and other plants. The adults feed on nectar from native plants.
- Habitat endemic to Hawaii, now limited to the islands of Maui, the Big Island, and Kaho'olawe. Found in coastal and dry forests at elevations from sea level to 5,000 feet.
- Threats include loss of habitat, nonnative ants, and parasitic wasps that prey on the eggs and caterpillars, and loss of the native host plant. This moth is overcollected by individuals for personal collections or for trade.
- The hope is that with the loss of the aiea, these insects will feed on nonnative plant species such as the tree tobacco and tomato plants. Note that the endangered aiea is also depicted on this quilt.

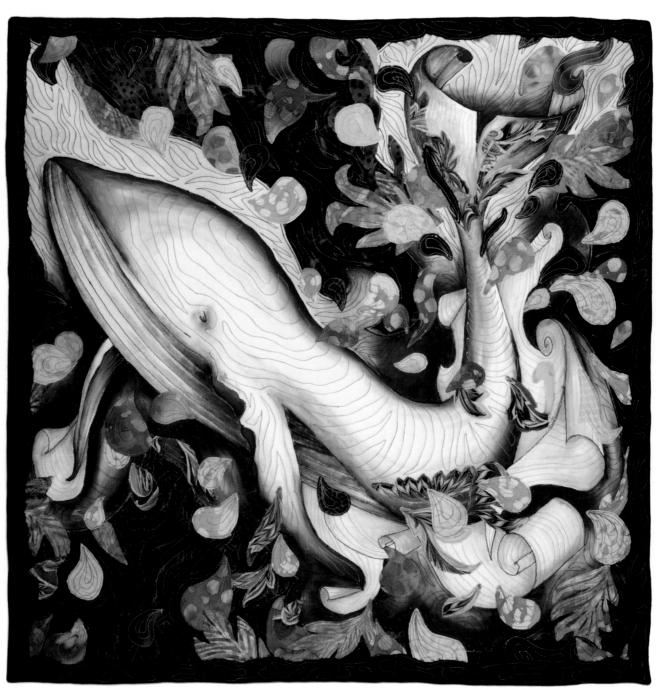

Pascale Michalski, Dartford, United Kingdom

BLUE WHALE

- *Balaenoptera musculus*
- Chordata/Mammalia
- Endangered: population trend increasing
- This whale has a long, tapered body with a flat, U-shaped head. Did you know the blue whale is the largest animal to have ever existed? Its tongue can weigh as much as an elephant, and its heart weighs around 400 pounds, according to National Geographic. They are 80 to 105 feet long, weigh up to 200 tons, and live for 80 to 90 years. Blue whales survive by eating krill, consuming 4 tons a day. They can swim 30 miles per hour, but their average rate is 12 miles per hour. They have been tracked to swim almost 300 miles in a day, and during migration, the depth at which they commonly swim is around 43 feet. They are solitary or travel in pairs. Calves weigh almost 6,000 pounds when they are born. And during the first seven months of life, a calf drinks 100 gallons of milk per day, gaining 200 pounds every 24 hours.
- Found in the North Atlantic and North Pacific Oceans.
- These creatures are in peril because of climate change and ship strikes. At one time, commercial whaling was a threat, but this is no longer the case because the species is protected.
- To save the blue whale, halt climate change and reduce pollution.

Starla Phelps, Alexandria, Virginia

BLUE-THROATED MACAW

- *Ara glaucogularis*
- Chordata/Aves
- Critically Endangered: population trend stable
- These birds are blue and green with a yellow chest. They have large, powerful beaks that can easily crack nuts and coconuts. Their dry, salty tongues contain a bone inside that makes them useful for tapping into fruits. The toes can grab branches, fruits, nuts, insects, and snails. The tails are very long. Macaws are social birds that mate for life and sleep in trees. Before 1990, no one even knew these birds existed.
- They are located in rainforests where there are green tree canopies and colorful fruits and flowers in northern parts of Bolivia, in South America. They are concentrated in swampy lowlands to savanna grasslands, east of the upper Rio Mamoré Beni.
- Macaws are playful, colorful, and beautiful. Because of this, they are popular pets and are illegally trapped for trade. Their rainforest homes are disappearing at an alarming rate. The area where these birds live is in the dairy-farming region of Bolivia, and the coconut trees, where the birds nest, are being cut down. Deforestation and poaching have put these macaws seriously at risk.
- Bolivia outlawed hunting and capture of the macaws, but without cooperation and enforcement, there is little hope. Extensive research is seeking solutions to their demise. In 2007 the American Bird Conservancy supported the expansion of protection of the nesting areas, which has helped somewhat. In 2015, the Bird Endowment began positioning boxes on trees to provide nesting places to encourage reproduction.

Lisa Chin, Salt Lake City, Utah

BOCACCIO ROCKFISH

- *Sebastes paucispinis*
- Chordata/Actinopterygii
- Critically Endangered
- These huge Pacific coast rockfish have a large mouth, an extended jaw, and mildly poisonous spines. They have an elongated body and are laterally compressed. Up to 3 feet in length, their life span is up to 50 years old. Adult coloration varies from shades of pink to pink brown, olive orange, brown, gray, or red, extending downward over the belly. They like rocky bottoms and prefer to live in water that is 160 to 820 feet deep. They are occasionally found in water over 1,500 feet. Adults move into deeper water as they age and grow.
- These fish are found along the northeastern Pacific Ocean, from the Gulf of Alaska to central Baja California in Mexico, but are most common between Oregon and northern Baja California.
- They are becoming extinct because of directed fishing, by catch in other fisheries, including those for salmon, and from adverse environmental factors.
- Various states have strict restrictions on how many of these fish can be caught per day. But because of the bocaccio's slow growth and long maturity, it may not be enough.

Laura Catherine Gilmartin, Stafford, Virginia

BORNEAN ORANGUTAN

- *Pongo pygmaeus*
- Chordata/Mammalia
- Critically Endangered: population decreasing
- This orangutan has very long arms, gray skin, and a coarse reddish coat. They can grasp with their hands and feet, and they are close relatives to humans.
- They are located in Malaysian Borneo, deep in the rainforests.
- Palm oil plantations are leading to loss of habitat. Other problems are hunting and forest fires.
- The rainforest habitat needs to be protected, and there should be regional land-use planning. Control logging and enforce hunting laws. The Great Projects is a group dedicated to preserve, educate, and save the orangutan and other endangered species. They offer tours to teach about and help preserve this species. Trained volunteers provide aid in the rehabilitation and release of these mammals.

Maria Wilkins, Bumpass, Virginia

- *Actenoides bougainville*
- Chordata/Aves
- Endangered: population trend decreasing
- This territorial bird is almost 12 inches long, with an orange-colored bill and purplish mustache, wings, tail, and back. They eat frogs and bugs, and they nest in holes in trees. Their call, "ko-ko-ko-ko," sounds like a loud laugh.

- Endemic to forests in the tropical to subtropical habitat of Bougainville Island in Papua, New Guinea
- Populations are declining due to predation by introduced rats and cats, and habitat degradation.
- To revive the species, the population needs to be surveyed. A system of community-based conservation areas should be established.

BRIDLED NAILTAIL WALLABY

Judy Grumbacher, Alexandria, Virginia

- *Onychogalea fraenata*
- Chordata/Mammalia
- Vulnerable: population stable
- Do you know the difference between a wallaby and a kangaroo? The main difference is size. A wallaby weighs up to 53 pounds and is just over 3 feet in length. A kangaroo can weigh 200 pounds and is 6 feet long. The distinguishing features of these wallabies are the white "bridle" line from the back of the neck to behind the forearms. The tail of this animal composes more than half its length, and there is a black spur on the tip. This wallaby has gray, yellowish, and white fur. It is nicknamed the "organ grinder" because when it runs away, it rotates its forearms.

- They are located in and around the Taunton National Scientific Park near Dingo in Queensland, Australia. Their habitat is in scrubland and grassy locations.
- The biggest threat to this species is competition for grazing areas. They compete for food with rabbits and are hunted by foxes and feral cats.
- Captive breeding programs are in action at Taunton National Scientific Park and at the Western Plains Zoo. Animals bred from these programs are being introduced back into the wild. There are plans to develop a backup colony at Dubbo in New South Wales.

Maggie Ward, Warrenton, Virginia

BUFFY-HEADED MARMOSET

- *Callithrix flaviceps*
- Chordata/Mammalia
- Endangered: population decreasing
- This tiny monkey is the most endangered of all the marmosets. They weigh 4 to 15 pounds and are around 10 inches long, not including their tail. They have a grayish body with buff-colored fur on the head and around the face. Their long tails are not prehensile; this means they cannot grasp with their tail.
- Found in the rainforests of Brazil
- They are at risk because their size makes them extremely vulnerable to predators. Their habitat is disappearing due to development, and they are hunted as pets.
- Several groups of these marmosets live on private, protected farmland and on an animal preserve. This provides some relief. Laws against ownership as pets would be beneficial.

BURROWING OWL

Claire Josiak, Calgary, Alberta, Canada

- *Athene cunicularia*
- Chordata/Aves
- Although IUCN lists this species of least concern, the US Forest Service indicates they are Endangered in Canada, Threatened in Mexico, and Endangered, Threatened, or of special concern in nine US States.
- At 9 inches in length, this is one of the smallest owl species. They are identified by long legs and a short, barred tail. The head, neck, and wings are light brown, with white streaks on the crown and larger spots on the back and wings. A light line extends under the throat, and the plumage is speckled.
- These owls live in abandoned burrows in open grassland. Their range is from southern Canada to South America, where they migrate.
- Pesticides and human encroachment are putting them at risk. As open grassland areas are cleared for development of homes, roads, golf courses, and airports, the owls are losing their natural habitat. Heavy rainstorms flood the burrows where the owls make their homes, and droughts cause the grasslands to dry up, making them unsuitable to sustain the owls. Climate change is troublesome.
- Protection programs such as the Recovery of Nationally Endangered Wildlife, Burrowing Owl Conservation Network, and the Migratory Bird Treaty Act (of Canada, the US, and Mexico) are beneficial. Reintroduction to native habitat, awareness, and protection are additional steps toward recovery.

CALIFORNIA CONDOR

Karen Mudry Avil, Great Falls, Virginia

- *Gymnogyps californianus*
- Chordata/Aves
- Critically Endangered: population increasing
- This is the largest North American land bird, and it has a life span of up to 60 years. These birds can weigh 25 pounds, and their wingspan is up to 9.8 feet. Feathers are black with some white on the undersides, and the head is mostly bald. The San Diego Zoo describes their "extraordinary eyesight, and an inquisitive and engaging intelligence. American tribes have great respect for the condor. . . . They call it the Thunderbird because they believe the bird brings thunder to the skies with the beating of its huge wings."

- Habitat is in California, Arizona, and Mexico
- At one time, there were thousands of these birds from California to Florida to New York. The population is at risk because of low clutch size, sexual maturity age, poaching, lead and DDT poisoning, electric power lines, egg collecting, and destruction of habitat.
- Their numbers are now increasing due to the California Condor Recovery Program. Once there were 23 birds, but now there are 446; the birds are being reintroduced into the wild. At last, more condors fly free in the wild than in captivity.

Dottie Dane, Annandale, Virginia

- *Ammodramus maritimus* subsp. *mirabilis*
- Chordata/Aves
- Classified as Endangered by the USFWS
- This subspecies is larger than most sparrows. Its large beak comes in handy for eating seeds, insects, beetles, and marine invertebrates. It is distinguished by a white throat, long tail, and yellow color above the eye. This is a nonmigratory bird. It is nicknamed "Goldilocks" because its habitat has to be "just right."
- They are found only in southern Florida, in a small section of the Everglades. They live along tidal creeks of salt marshes in the reeds and rushes and seek open areas. Since they nest close to the ground, they do not like flooded or over-vegetated locations.
- Hurricanes have caused a change in the habitat, causing the bird to move north from the original Florida location, Cape Sable. Hurricanes and the water management practice of draining South Florida have increased the water levels, causing habitat destruction. Lawsuits are threatened to halt or change the water drainage that is flooding the western Everglades.
- To save this species, legislation or more interest in stopping water flow to the western Everglades from other parts of Florida is necessary. The Everglades Restoration Transition Plan aims to improve these conditions.

CAPE SEAHORSE

Diane Tansey Cairns, Springfield, Virginia

- *Hippocampus capensis*
- Chordata/Actinopterygii
- Endangered: population trend decreasing
- These seahorses, less than 5 inches in length, inhabit mainly tropical and temperate coastal waters. They eat shrimp, small fish, and plankton. They are chameleonlike since they can change colors to blend into their surroundings. Life span is five to seven years.
- Endemic to waters off South Africa

- Some cultures believe seahorses have magical powers, and they are used in Chinese medicine. They are becoming diminished because of the illegal trade for ornamental display in aquariums.
- To revive this species, marine protected areas must be supported along coastlines. Stop deforestation in marine waters, reduce ocean pollution, and inform the public so they will refuse to purchase them for aquariums.

Susan M. Bynum, Falls Church, Virginia

- *Remphastidae vitellinus*
- Chordata/Aves
- Vulnerable: population trend decreasing
- There are 35 to 40 different species of toucans, which are varied in size and color. On the basis of the loud noises they make, these are either "croakers" or "yelpers." The channel-billed toucans are "yelpers." At 19 inches long, they are mostly black with some red and yellow/orange/white on their throats, and their beaks are black. They fly poorly because they don't have capable wingspans; they get around best by hopping. They live mostly in the tops of the canopy and eat fruits, nuts, insects, and small lizards.

- These birds are found in forests and woodlands on the island of Trinidad and in tropical South America, in the southeastern Amazon, and as far south as southern Brazil and central Bolivia.
- Their numbers are steadily declining because of accelerating deforestation. Land is being cleared for cattle ranching and soy production, facilitated by expansion of roads. They are also at risk due to hunting.
- To protect toucans, conserve rainforests, and make it illegal to capture, trade, or sell their body parts, including their feathers and beaks.

CHEETAH

Diane L. Azzaline Murtha, Bettendorf, Iowa

- *Acinonyx jubatus*
- Chordata/Mammalia
- Vulnerable: population trend decreasing
- Typically yellowish tan, the coat of the cheetah is uniformly covered with nearly 2,000 solid black spots. It is light and slender compared to the other big cats. Their superpower is they are the fastest land animal, averaging 40 miles per hour when sprinting, with bursts of speed reaching 70 miles per hour.

- They are located in forests and savannas in eastern and southern Africa.
- The species is declining due to excessive hunting and poaching, habitat loss, and illegal pet trade.
- Stronger enforcement of endangered species and antipoaching laws are in dire need.

Holly Cole, Triangle, Virginia

CHIMPANZEE

- *Pan troglodytes*
- Chordata/Mammalia
- Endangered: population trend decreasing
- Chimpanzees share approximately 98 percent of our DNA, making them our closest living relatives in the animal kingdom. The males weigh 88 to 132 pounds, and females weigh 70 to 104 pounds. They have large ears, sleep in nests in trees at night, and are mostly black; males and females have a white beard. They feed on fruit, nuts, seeds, tree bark, plant bulbs and shoots, flowers, insects, and small animals
- They are located in West and Central Equatorial Africa: Sierra Leone, Angola, Congo, Senegal, Uganda, and Tanzania. Dense tropical rainforests are their preferred habitat. They can be found in secondary-growth forests, woodlands, bamboo forests, swamps, and the open savanna.
- The number of chimps has dwindled due to poaching and capture for the pet trade, habitat loss and rampant deforestation, local warfare, disease, and use in disease research. Only 21 percent are sheltered in national parks and reserves.
- In the US, contributions to funding for the Humane Society and National Institutes of Health create more refuges to support chimps that have been retired from scientific research. The Jane Goodall Institute, an organization that focuses on conserving habitat, rescuing chimp orphans, supporting law enforcement in protected areas, and raising awareness with communities and policymakers, is in need of contributions. Another Jane Goodall project that accepts donations is ChimpanZoo, an international program dedicated to the well-being and understanding of chimpanzees in zoos.

Vanessa McCallum, Murfreesboro, Tennessee

CHINESE ALLIGATOR

- *Alligator sinesis*
- Chordata/Reptilia
- Critically Endangered
- This is a small, stout, dark-green or black alligator, weighing up to 79 pounds and measuring almost 5 feet. This species is thought to be the basis of the mythical Chinese dragon. It is considered a living fossil, with relatives that date back over 200 million years. This alligator has a heavily scaled back and tail and an armored belly, with short legs and webbed feet. Shy, it lives in foliage at the shore of slow-moving water, where it hunts for small animals, mussels, fish, and frogs. They use their snout and front feet to burrow into streambanks, where they hibernate for as much as half a year. They move in and out of the water to regulate their temperature. In the wild, they have a 50-year life span. Do you know the difference between an alligator and a crocodile? The main difference is the shape of their snouts. Crocodiles have a pointier, V-shaped snout, and when their jaws are shut, their teeth are visible on the sides. Alligators have wider, U-shaped snouts.
- They live in still-water wetlands within the river basin of the Yangtze River in China.
- Even though they are nonaggressive toward humans, these alligators are seen as a menace, and people exterminate them, which is one of the reasons they are endangered. In addition, they are victims of agricultural chemical pollution and secondary poisoning.
- The alligators are being raised in zoos and breeding centers and have been successfully released into the wild.

Lynn Chinnis, Oro Valley, Arizona

- *Echinocereus chisosensis*
- Plantae/Cactaceae family
- Endangered: population trend decreasing
- Unique cacti of individual plants with 10 to 17 radial spines with a knobby stem surface. Its pinkish-magenta flowers contain hairlike spines.
- Grows at low elevations within Big Bend National Park in the Chihuahuan shrublands and in grasslands in gravelly soil.
- The species is at risk for many reasons, in particular because of infestation of nonnative buffelgrass and because of illegal collection, and the cacti are eaten by rodents.
- Conservation efforts include close monitoring by the National Park Service and the Fish and Wildlife Service.

Coelacanth

Kim Gibson, Burke, Virginia

- *Latimeria chalumnae*
- Chordata/Sarcopterygii
- Critically Endangered
- This prehistoric creature was believed to be extinct along with dinosaurs until its surprising rediscovery in 1938. It can grow up to 6.5 feet and 198 pounds and has a life span of up to 60 years. They prefer the deep sea and live in depths to 2,300 feet. Unusual characteristics include a hinged joint in the jaw, extraordinarily thick scales, and paired lobed fins that move in an alternating pattern, almost like legs.

- Found in the Comoros Islands near the east coast of Africa and off the coast of Indonesia.
- It is unknown exactly why they are so rare, but gill nets and deep-sea fishing are sources of mortality.
- Fishing methods must be changed to avoid gill nets, and fishing must be halted in the habitat of the coelacanth. Fishermen in the Comoros Islands are already voluntarily cooperating.

COMMON SPINY LOBSTER

Beth Shafer, Fairfax, Virginia

- *Palinurus elephas*
- Arthropoda/Malacostraca
- Vulnerable: population decreasing
- Most often 10 to 12 inches long, these lobsters are reddish brown with yellow spots. They are nocturnal scavengers and eat dead animals, worms, and crabs. Moray eels and nurse sharks eat them. During the daytime they hide in caves and rocks. They may live 50 years or longer.
- Occur in the eastern Atlantic Ocean, from Norway to Morocco, throughout the central part of the Mediterranean, the Canary Islands, and the Azores.
- Meat from these creatures is considered a delicacy. Populations are decreasing because fisheries overexploit them. Recreational and commercial fishing is in excess.
- Regulations should be established and enforced regarding size limits, type and number of fishing gear allowed, and closing entire seasons to fishing activity, and marine protected areas should be established.

CONSERVANCY FAIRY SHRIMP

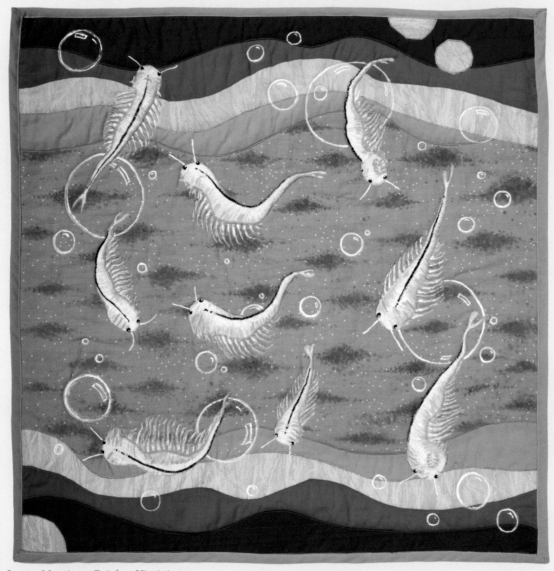

Lynne Morrison, Fairfax, Virginia

- *Branchinecta conservatio*
- Arthropoda/Branchiopoda
- Endangered
- This is a tiny aquatic crustacean, less than an inch long. They live in large turbid pools of cool water and in temporary rainwater pools.
- Mainly located in California

- Encroaching development is putting these shrimp at risk of extinction.
- Protect natural wetlands that support populations, curb urban development, and control the water supply and flood control projects.

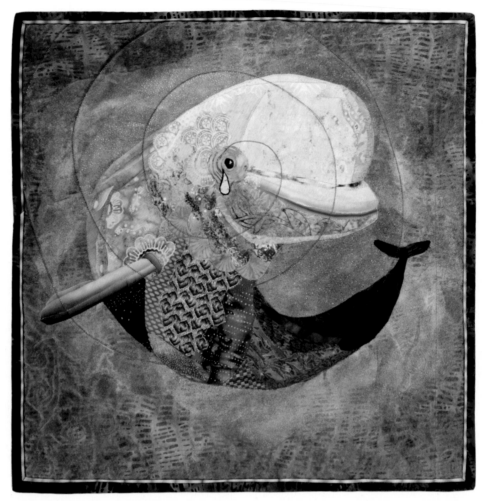

Andrea Harles, Washington, DC

- *Delphinapterus leucas*
- Chordata/Mammalia
- A new subpopulation in Cook Inlet was recently discovered and is listed as Critically Endangered on the IUCN Red List.
- Their average weight is 3,150 pounds, and they are 11 to 16 feet in length. Newborns weigh almost 160 pounds. These social animals are distinguished by their white color; they have a large, rounded head with a prominent forehead, which aids in producing and focusing sounds they make. They are called "canaries of the sea" because of the wide range of sounds they produce: whistling, squealing, mooing, chirping, and clicking. They have keen senses of sight and hearing. Their diet consists of fish, octopus, squid, and a broad range of shellfish. Because their cervical vertebrae are not fused, they can move their heads up and down and side to side, unusual in whales.

Their bodies are covered with a thick layer of blubber for protection and storing energy.

- They live only in Cook Inlet, a body of water south of Anchorage, Alaska, and this subpopulation does not migrate.
- Climate change is affecting their Arctic environment. Places to feed and to find protection from predators, including killer whales, are diminishing. Noise pollution in the ocean from oil and gas drilling adversely affect their existence by disturbing their ability to communicate.
- As part of the effort to save this species, the National Oceanic and Atmospheric Administration reports that yearly aerial surveys as well as surveys from shore are ongoing. Scientists listen for the whales with passive acoustics, and drones are collecting imagery to gather information on their health and to identify new calves.

CORPSE FLOWER

Judy Anderson, Fairfax, Virginia

- *Rafflesia arnoldii*
- Plantae/Rafflesiaceae family
- Not evaluated by the IUCN Red List, but the World Wildlife Fund reports this species as Endangered.
- These plants contain the world's largest and heaviest individual flowers. They are leathery red, brown, and orange with cream-colored spots, consisting of five large petals, but have no stems, leaves, or true roots. The flowers can grow up to 3 feet wide and weigh up to 24 pounds. It is a parasitic plant and smells like a rotting corpse; this odor attracts flies and beetles, which transport the pollen.

- Grow mainly in India
- Population continues to fall due to the decline in the extent and quality of their habitat. Roads are being built on the mountain where they are found, and the lower mountain slopes are being converted into banana plantations, causing further encroachment.
- Their habitat must be preserved and improved in order to sustain the few that remain.

Laura Catherine Gilmartin, Stafford, Virginia

- *Felis concolor* subsp. *costaricensis*
- Chordata/Mammalia
- Designated Endangered by Environmental Conservation Online System (www.ecos.fws.gov), US Fish & Wildlife Service; the population is declining.
- This puma weighs between 55 to 150 pounds. Males tend to be significantly larger than females. Its coloring is light brown. Very little information is available on this subspecies.
- Endemic to Costa Rica

- There has been widespread killing by people trying to protect livestock. Habitat loss, population decline, and subsequent inbreeding resulted in significant loss of genetic variability and overall deterioration of health.
- There is a sanctuary in Costa Rica.

CUBAN CROCODILE

Janet Palfey, Fairfax, Virginia

- *Crocodylus rhombifer*
- Chordata/Reptilia
- Critically Endangered
- Green and olive black with yellow markings, this is the most colorful crocodile species. It is also the one with the longest legs, which makes it the fastest one on land. They are proficient both on land and in the water. They can grow up to 10.5 feet, which means they are slightly smaller than other crocs; they feed on small mammals.

- Endemic to Cuba, found in tropical freshwater swamps
- They are at risk because of habitat loss and hybridization with other species, and they are hunted; their meat is popular both with locals and tourists.
- Cuba captured and released this reptile to a nature preserve, the Zapata Swamp, in the 1960s. The American species should be kept apart from the Cuban crocodile.

Debbie Dempsey, Oak Hill, Virginia

CUBAN PAINTED SNAIL

- *Polymita picta*
- Chordata/Mollusca
- Not evaluated by the IUCN Red List; declared endangered by the Encyclopedia of Life
- These tiny jewels are less than an inch in diameter, and they are considered the most beautiful terrestrial snail in the world. "Polymita" describes their unique features: many stripes. Legend says a lovely Indian girl was adored by an Indian chief. To win her love, the chief set out to capture the yellow of the sun, the green of the meadows, the brown of the mountains, the pink of the flowers, and the white foam at the crest of the waves. But night caught him unexpectedly, and the blue of the sky eluded him. This is the reason why *polymitas* are said to exhibit every shade of the rainbow except for blue. The snails prefer subtropical, humid environments that ensure growth of plenty of food: fungi, lichen, mushrooms, and moss. They clean their host plants, and photosynthesis is facilitated. Their life span is just over a year.
- Endemic to Cuba, these snails live on the leaves and trunks of different plants, including coffee bushes and coconut trees, in a geographical area on the southeastern coast from mountains to sea, in one of the most biologically diverse ecosystems in the world.
- The exquisite beauty of the shells of these snails has made them a prime target for collectors, who pluck them from trees, destroying their habitat and decimating their population. The shells are used to make jewelry and trinkets. Natural predators include rats and the hook-billed kite.
- Conservation efforts include being declared a protected species since 1943 by Cuban legislation prohibiting export, except for scientific uses. Some specimen were successfully bred recently in a laboratory in Havana's Quinta de los Molinos, then were released into the wild.

Tammi Sparks, Sherman, Texas

DAMA GAZELLE

- *Nanger dama*
- Chordata/Mammalia
- Critically Endangered: population trend decreasing
- At 88 to 190 pounds, this is the largest gazelle. They are 39 inches in height to their shoulders and have a reddish-brown upper body and a white rump and underbelly. Their horns curve up and back. Diurnal, they have long legs and are well adapted to stay cool in the desert. Superpower: at just one week of age, a baby gazelle is able to run as fast as adults, 30 to 35 miles per hour. Do you know what pronking is? It is the word used to describe the way animals such as gazelles arch their backs, and with stiff legs, all four off the ground at once, they spring into the air.
- Located in African grasslands and in the Sahara Desert.
- Species is at risk because of excessive hunting. Rising population of domestic stock is competing for the same food. Climate change is causing important food sources (grass and trees) to stop growing.
- Reintroduction programs are necessary to get this species back into the wild. Create and enforce laws and punishments for hunters and poachers.

DAVIS' GREEN PITAYA

Polly Maynard Davis, Warrenton, Virginia

- *Echinocereus viridiflorus* subsp. *davisii*
- Plantae/Cactaceae family
- Endangered, according to the USFWS
- This plant is a dwarf single-stem cactus. It matures in three to four years, and in late March to early April it blooms. Flowers are yellowish green and are almost the same size as the plant.
- Endemic to Brewster County, in West Texas, in the Chihuahuan Desert.

- Problems facing this cactus are overcollection, encroaching plants, and possible habitat loss to mineral and oil exploration and extraction.
- The land encompassing this habitat has been privately purchased. The cacti are now protected because collection by enthusiasts is prohibited.

DEVIL'S HOLE PUPFISH

Diane Dresdner, Chantilly, Virginia

- *Cyprinodon diabolis*
- Chordata/Actinopterygii
- Critically Endangered: population decreasing
- This is a blue, iridescent, 1-inch-long fish that has adapted to harsh conditions of its habitat for thousands of years. This has made them a scientific wonder, but so vulnerable to extinction.
- Found in Ash Meadows National Wildlife Refuge in Nye County, Nevada, a detached unit of Death Valley National Park
- Populations are decreasing because of changes in the environment; scientists are working to understand the changes. In 1976, a presidential proclamation was issued to establish Devil's Hole as a national monument, and water rights necessary to preserve the monument, including preservation of its pool and fish, were reserved.
- Continue to feed pupfish in Devil's Hole and increase early-life-state pupfish by using artificial and natural cover to help them hide. Work is being done with some success at a new facility where the Ash Meadows Fish Conservation Facility accepts eggs and adult pupfish to establish an additional population outside Devil's Hole.

Diane Dresdner, Chantilly, Virginia

- *Erythrolamprus atraventer*
- Chordata/Reptilia
- Vulnerable: population decreasing
- Small and bright green in color, not much information is available on this species.
- Endemic to Brazil rainforest areas in Rio de Janeiro and Sao Paolo
- Habitat is at risk because of deforestation for homes and agriculture. Prized by reptile enthusiasts for their size and color.
- Land and water protection and management need to be heightened, and collectors must be deterred. Education is required for species management and to improve their habitat.

DWARF BEARCLAW POPPY

Sylvia Borschel Lewis, Kanab, Utah

- *Arctomecon humilis*
- Plantae/Papaveraceae family
- Not evaluated by IUCN Red List, listed as Critically Imperiled by NatureServe
- A perennial herb that grows in a circular rosette low to the ground. Found only on gypsum soil.
- Located in Washington County, Utah

- This species suffers from loss of habitat due to urban development, and trail use by humans.
- Protect habitat from urban development and degradation. Support pollinators. Perform propagation research.

Nancy L. Evans, Jeffersonton, Virginia

ELEGANT SUNBIRD

- *Aethopyga duyvenbodei*
- Chordata/Aves
- Endangered: population decreasing
- This bird is less than 5 inches in size. The male is more colorful and has metallic green/blue patches on the crown and upper parts of the wings, a red collar of feathers, a yellow-olive back and bright-yellow underparts, and a band on the rump. It has a thin curved beak. The birds were once forest dependent but are now seen in areas of scrub and plantations, close to forests near hardwood trees.
- Species is confined to the Indonesian island of Sangihe, on Mount Sahendaruman.
- The forest on Sangihe has almost been cleared of fruit, spices, and fiber, due to plantations and their harvest of rubber, coconuts, teas, and bananas. Only tiny patches of forest remain. Agriculture destroys the understory and scrub, which the elegant sunbird requires for its habitat.
- The Action Sampiri Project provides conservation awareness programs and aims to have land-use agreements with interested parties. There are plans to reclassify a local forest as a wildlife reserve, which would be beneficial to the sunbirds.

Nancy B. Adams, Annandale, Virginia; Karen Wolfson, Chantilly, Virginia

ESKIMO CURLEW

- *Numenius borealis*
- Chordata/Aves
- Critically Endangered
- Medium-sized shorebird with a long, slender bill that curves downward. Notable black V-shaped marks are on the body, and the legs are bluish gray. They consume berries before migration and eat insects on their flight back north.
- These birds breed in the tundra of the far Northwest Territory of Canada and possibly in Alaska. They migrate far south for the winter, traveling more than 9,000 miles to the southernmost parts of South America.
- Years ago, these curlews were excessively hunted, which was believed to be the cause of population decline. However, when hunting them was outlawed, the population did not revive. Other reasons for their decline include loss of prairies to agriculture, suppression of wildfires, and the extinction of a valuable food source, the Rocky Mountain grasshopper. These factors not only affected their breeding grounds but progressed to their wintering grounds, making it even more difficult for populations to be recovered.
- Unfortunately, there has not been a confirmed sighting since 1963, but there have been unconfirmed sightings. Public education and captive breeding would be beneficial, but the challenge is finding surviving specimens. The only option currently in place is the conservation of historical breeding and wintering grounds. Observation and monitoring are recommended rather than interference.

Hollis Olson, Lovettsville, Virginia

- *Euphorbia cap-saintemariensis* (there is no common name)
- Plantae/Euphorbiaceae family
- Critically Endangered
- This is an interesting miniature plant with many branching silver-gray stems that spread from a tuberous root. It grows in rock cracks or under plants on windy terrain, where its branches grow horizontally, close to the ground. This succulent has small, cup-shaped, yellow-pink flowers at the end of the stems.
- They are found only on the southern tip of Madagascar, about 328 feet above sea level in an area of about 110 by 980 yards.
- They are becoming extinct because of their limited distribution and the small area where they exist. Their habitat is experiencing degradation due in part to natural disasters and wildfires. The plants are collected by horticulturists.
- To conserve the species, the population in the Cap Sainte-Marie needs continued protection; the listing under CITES should be maintained.

EUROPEAN EEL

Suzanne Meader, Sterling, Virginia

- *Anguilla anguilla*
- Chordata/Actinopterygii
- Critically Endangered: population trend decreasing
- The eel has an elongated body; females can be up to 5 feet in length, and males grow to about 20 inches long. They have a dorsal fin that runs along the length of their bodies, and their gills are located in a pouch on both sides of their heads. They spend their days under stones and in crevices, skittering along the bottoms of rivers, lakes, and ponds, but are most active at night. They migrate to the sea to spawn, and after breeding and laying their eggs, they die. They eat almost any small animal, both alive and dead, and cannibalism is common in crowded areas. They are prey to fish-eating birds and mammals, and they are a favorite entrée of otters.
- It is believed they spawn in the Sargasso Sea before migrating to bodies of water in Europe.
- Extinction is threatened because of overfishing, pollution, parasites, and hydroelectric power plants.
- To revive the species, there should be a prohibition on fisheries, and management of the migratory passage through man-made industrial river obstacles.

Ricki Selva, Fort Myer, Virginia

- *Trichechus manatus* subsp. *latirostris*
- Chordata/Mammalia
- Vulnerable: population trend decreasing
- Florida's state marine mammal is a large aquatic relative of the elephant. They are grayish brown and have thick, wrinkled skin on which there is often a growth of algae. Their front flippers help them steer, or sometimes crawl, through shallow water. They have powerful, flat tails to propel them through the water. Despite small eyes and a lack of outer ears, they see and hear quite well. They can reach lengths of 13 feet and weigh as much as 1,300 pounds.
- They are located throughout the Caribbean basin, including the southeastern US, eastern Mexico, eastern Central America, northeastern South America, and the Greater Antilles.

- Manatees are in jeopardy because of collisions with boats and loss of warmwater springs that provide critical habitat. Their reproductive rates are low, and they are vulnerable to entanglement in fishing gear, red tide, and algal blooms. They are experiencing loss of food sources and seagrass beds due to pollutants. Other dangers include cold weather, tropical storms and hurricanes, tidal entrapments, and disease.
- To revive the species, minimize causes of manatee disturbance, harassment, injury, and mortality. Determine and monitor the status of the population. Identify, assess, and reduce human-related manatee mortality. Minimize alteration, degradation, and destruction of habitats and protect these areas. Facilitate manatee recovery through public awareness and education.

FLORIDA PANTHER

Lois Ann Borlase, The Villages, Florida

- *Puma concolor* subsp. *coryi*
- Chordata/Mammalia
- According to the IUCN Red List, this panther subspecies living in Florida is a remnant subpopulation that persists and is Endangered; Defenders of Wildlife says it is one of the most endangered mammals on Earth: population trend decreasing.
- This is a subspecies of cougar that has adapted to a subtropical environment. It is tan with lighter fur on the lower chest, belly, and inner legs. Panthers are more closely related to small cats (such as the lynx and house cat) than to big cats such as lions and tigers. They do not roar, and they are solitary. Adult males may range 200 square miles, females range 70 to 80 square miles. They can swim and have a keen sense of smell. They are efficient hunters that prefer live prey, mostly deer, wild hogs, and raccoons.
- They are located in the southern tip of Florida, south of the Caloosahatchee River and the Everglades area.

Pinelands, hardwood hammocks, and mixed swamp forests are their usual habitat.
- They are at risk because males stake out home ranges; habitat is being lost due to development. Roadkill presents a danger; 34 panthers were killed by vehicles in 2016. Other problems include inbreeding of shrinking population, which is leading to genetic weakness, and mercury contamination by raccoons in the Everglades.
- To save the panthers, protect their habitat. This will require aggressive protection of the remaining wildlands in South Florida, and conservation efforts on private lands. Panthers from Texas were introduced in Florida to provide more genetic variety and to help the population increase. Wildlife crossings established under heavily traveled roadways are helpful, as is breeding panthers in captivity and then releasing them into the wild.

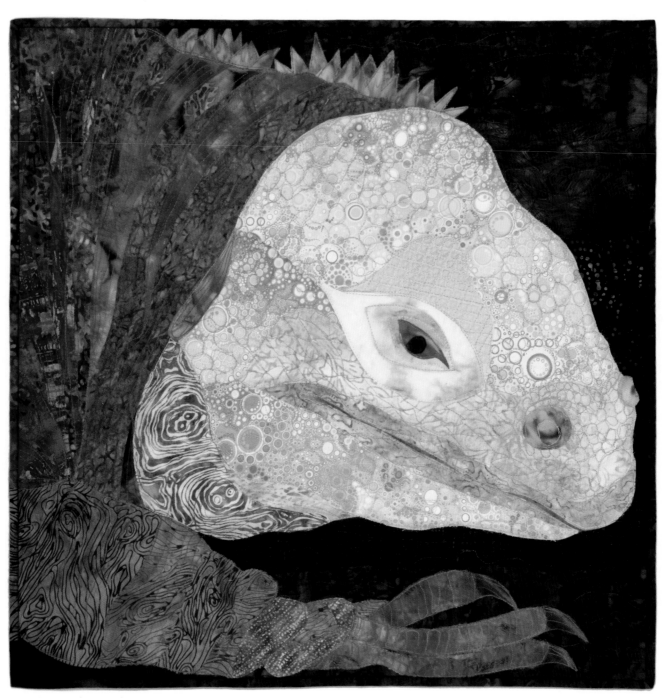

Susan Fernandez, Fairfax Station, Virginia

Galápagos Land Iguana

- *Conolophus subcristatus*
- Chordata/Reptilia
- Vulnerable
- This large, yellow lizard, which measures just over 3 feet in length, is reminiscent of a dragon. It is covered in scales with a spiky crest along the neck and back. A herbivore that feeds mostly on prickly pear leaves and fruit, it has thick, powerful back legs and long, sharp claws on its toes. If they survive the first few precarious years of life, when they are most vulnerable to predators and food scarcity, these iguanas can live up to 50 years.
- They are one of three iguana species endemic to the Galápagos Islands, Ecuador. They live in dry, scrubby terrains.
- The introduction of predators such as dogs and cats and other domestic animals (e.g., pigs and goats) has caused the population to be threatened and nearly eradicated. Cats prey on their eggs and on young iguanas up to four years of age, and domestic animals destroy their food source.
- The Charles Darwin Research Station and the Galápagos National Park Service conducted an emergency rescue of 60 remaining survivors in 1976 on Santa Cruz. They established a captive breeding program on Santa Cruz Island that continues today. Young iguanas are returned to the wild when they reach a size considered safe from cat predation. Other measures include eradication and control of introduced animals, maintenance of their habitat, and continued monitoring of populations.

Terry Kramzar, Kennett Square, Pennsylvania

GHOST ORCHID

- *Dendrophylas lendeuii*
- Plantae/Orchidaceae family
- Not evaluated by the IUCN Red List; listed as Endangered by the NPS
- This plant has white to cream-colored blooms approximately 1 inch long, flowering on leafless stems in marshy, deep swamps of cypress and palm trees.
- Found in Cuba, in the Bahamas, and at Everglades National Park, Big Cypress Preserve, and Corkscrew Swamp Sanctuary, and in the wild in Florida.
- Species is in peril because of habitat destruction. Hydraulic changes have resulted from urban development. Other problems include loss of pollinators, use of pesticides, climate change, and overcollecting by poachers who are removing plants from their natural environment.
- Protected in many public land areas in southern Florida. New restoration techniques are being developed to culture plants from seeds in the lab and acclimatize them to greenhouses by botanists at the University of Florida. This has produced mature seedlings for habitat field establishment.

Willa Downes, Fairfax, Virginia

- *Tridacna gigas*
- Chordata/Mollusca
- Vulnerable: population declining
- This is the largest living bivalve and the heaviest mollusk. They grow to more than 4 feet long and can weigh 650 pounds.
- Habitat is coral reefs, within 65 feet of the surface, in shallow waters of the Pacific from Thailand and Japan to Australia and Micronesia.
- Numbers are falling because they are overharvested as food, and they are prized and acquired by the aquarium trade as an exotic specimen.
- Attempts are being made to raise them at clam hatcheries, after which they are reintroduced back into the wild.

Giant Panda

Nicki Allen, Springfield, Virginia

- *Ailuropoda melanoleuca*
- Chordata/Mammalia
- Vulnerable: population trend increasing
- Large black and white bear, between 4 to 6 feet long and weighing 175 to 280 pounds. Vegetarians, pandas eat 88 pounds of bamboo a day. They are solitary and do not hibernate. Good tree climbers, their enemies are Asian golden cats, tigers, panthers, jackals, wolves, and marten. Their life span in captivity is up to 30 years.

- Live in temperate broadleaf and mixed forests of southwestern China.
- Poaching and deforestation in the 1980s led these animals to be listed as Endangered in 1990.
- China has worked to conserve the habitat of giant pandas. There are 67 panda reserves in China. Due to tireless efforts of conservationists and the country's efforts at reforestation, farmland expansion, and panda reserves, the giant panda was recently moved from Endangered to Vulnerable status.

GINKGO

Nancy Daprile Jones, Woodbridge, Virginia

- *Ginkgo biloba* (also called maidenhair tree)
- Plantae/Ginkgoaceae family
- Endangered
- These slow-growing trees are widely used as a source of food in Asia, and they are used in traditional medicine. At 66 to 115 feet tall, some are said to be more than 2,500 years old. The unique fan-shaped leaves turn bright golden yellow in the fall. A superpower is their surprising adaptability to many varied conditions. Ginkgo biloba trees that grew approximately a mile from where the Hiroshima atom bomb exploded were among the few survivors. In fact, they are still alive today.
- Grown initially in China and Tibetan gardens, they are cultivated worldwide in broadleaved forest environments.
- They are endangered because they are rare in the wild.
- Conservation efforts include plans for continued cultivation, use of microcuttings, and standardizing the use of ginkgo extract.

Charla J. Viehe, Hoover, Alabama

- *Giraffa camelopardali* subsp. *peralta*
- Chordata/Mammalia
- Vulnerable: population trend decreasing
- Giraffes are light tan with light reddish-brown spots of various shapes and sizes. At 18 feet tall, they are the world's tallest animal. A giraffe can go longer periods of time without water than a camel. Their tongue can measure 21 inches in length. These iconic herbivores munch on the tops of trees. Social and nomadic, they live and migrate in small groups of 15 to 20, called "towers." Affection is shown by rubbing heads. They can run up to 35 miles per hour when chased by predators such as lions, hyenas, wild dogs, and leopards. Young giraffes are especially vulnerable to predators; only half survive to adulthood. A superpower they have is the ability to crush the head of a predator with a kick of their strong legs.

- Their native habitats are savannas, grasslands, and the dry woodlands of sub-Saharan Africa. Only a small population of the West African giraffe subspecies remains in southwestern Niger; all individuals of this subspecies are in the wild; none are in zoos.
- Populations have declined due to habitat loss, human encroachment, political unrest, poor land use and planning, legal hunting, and poaching. Their tails are prized in many African cultures, and they are desired for their meat and pelts.
- To save this species, there should be governmental involvement in land acquisition and planning for human development, the establishment of habitat parks and safe zones, and the planting of acacia, mimosa, and wild apricot plants. Other solutions are necessary to feed hungry people, illegal hunting practices need to be policed, and cultural and livelihood practices involving giraffe parts must be changed.

Golden Lion Tamarin

Susie Goodman, Bloomington, Indiana

- *Leontopithecus rosalia*
- Chordata/Mammalia
- Endangered: population stable
- These are small monkeys weighing 17 to 24 ounces, measuring 6 to 10 inches, and having a 12-to-15-inch prehensile (adapted for grasping) tail. They have a striking reddish-gold coat with a long, backswept mane.
- They live in the Atlantic coastal rainforest of southeastern Brazil in the midlevel tree canopy.
- Their endangered status results from severe habitat loss, fragmentation, and collection for the pet trade.
- To help revive the species, support the Association of Zoos and Aquarium Species Survival Plan and specifically support the Smithsonian's National Zoo and Conservation Biology Institute and the International Committee for Conservation and Management of the Golden Lion Tamarin.

Cheryl Rounds, Vienna, Virginia

- *Guaruba guarouba* (also commonly called golden conure)
- Chordata/Aves
- Vulnerable: population trend decreasing
- Medium-sized parrot, around 13 inches. Plumage is mainly rich yellow with dark-green secondary wings, and they have a large, grayish-colored bill. They eat fruit and plants. These social birds help other pairs of golden parakeets care for their young birds.
- They are endemic to the rainforests of Brazil.

- The species is declining from deforestation and flooding, causing a loss of their natural habitat. Toucans prey upon helpless nestlings.
- They are protected under Brazilian law, but restrictions on trade need to be enforced. Ensure protections of the Gurupi Biological Reserve. Conduct searches for any possible undiscovered populations.

Maria Janotkova, Bratislava, Slovakia

Goldstreifiger

- *Buprestis splendens* (also known as jewel beetles)
- Arthropoda/Insecta
- Endangered: population decreasing
- Because of their iridescence, these terrestrial bugs are named after prismatic shells. They eat and live in dead wood.
- Endemic to Europe
- Larvae development occurs in large tree trunks that are in the sun. Due to the removal of old-growth trees by logging companies, these beetles are vulnerable to forest fires and predators. They are popular with beetle collectors.
- Protected officially under the Bern Convention and European Habitats Directive, there is a need to increase land management of old-growth trees. Populations could improve if sites where they are found are monitored, and if more is done to conserve forests. Restrict collection.

Lisa Arthaud, Warrenton, Virginia

Grandidier's Baobab Tree

- *Adansonia grandidieri*
- Plantae/Malvaceae family
- Endangered: population decreasing
- Massive cylindrical trunks help this tree overcome drought by storing water; their superpower is that the trunk diameter fluctuates. This is the largest and best known of several types of baobabs. Leaves appear from October through May. White flowers, smelling of sour watermelon, open near dusk from May through August. The tree bears ripe fruit in November and December.
- Endemic to Madagascar in dry deciduous forests, close to bodies of water
- Threats include intense deforestation due to the expansion of human migration and agriculture. The species has a low regeneration rate. Livestock graze on its seedlings, humans consume its fruit and collect the seeds, and it is used to manufacture cosmetics.
- There are currently no laws to control exploitation of this plant.

Sherri Cyra, Middleton, Wisconsin

Green Peafowl

- *Pavo muticus*
- Chordata/Aves
- Endangered: population trend decreasing
- This lesser-known peafowl is larger than the common blue-plumed variety and is one of the largest game birds. They are known primarily for their distinctive and iridescent body and train feathers. Females are more colorful than their blue cousins, but they lack the colorful train of the male. The green peafowl has a more upright neck and posture than other peafowls.
- Their habitat is fragmented, and they are believed to already be extinct in some areas of South Asia. Populations still exist in Cambodia, Myanmar, and Vietnam. Smaller populations can be found in western and northern Thailand, in parts of China, southern Laos, and Java in Indonesia.
- The primary threats are high hunting levels and conversion of habitat. The birds are hunted for their feathers and meat; eggs and chicks are also collected. As land is developed for human use, habitat is lost and access to water is negatively affected. Farmers consider peafowls to be pests, so pesticides are used to poison them.
- The species would benefit from enforcing hunting and trade bans, pesticide regulations, expansion of protected habitats and breeding programs, and increased public education. Multiple South Asian countries have established wildlife sanctuaries, nature preserves, and conservancy areas in an effort to stabilize the green peafowl.

Carole A. Nicholas, Oakton, Virginia

HAWKSBILL TURTLE

- *Eretmochelys imbricata*
- Chordata/Reptilia
- Critically Endangered: population decreasing
- This turtle has a beautifully patterned shell, a narrow head, and jaws like a hawk's beak. This allows the turtle to get food from small crevices in coral reefs. Of the seven species of sea turtles, this one is relatively small, growing to a maximum of 45 inches in length and 150 pounds in weight. Their life span is 30 to 50 years. This species is omnivorous. Their favorite food is sea sponges, and they eat jellyfish, anemones, sea urchins, squid, shrimp, mollusks, marine algae, and fish. They have a superpower fairly recently discovered; in the Solomon Islands, this is the first reptile found to have bioflourescence. This means they have an ability to reflect blue light and reemit it as another color. Scientists are trying to determine whether this ability is for mating, for camouflage, to communicate, as a defense, or something entirely different. The study of fluorescence is important in helping scientists understand the way cells work; this could aid medical research and possibly the study of cancer.
- Their habitat is tropical coral reefs in the Atlantic, Indian, and Pacific Oceans. Mature females come ashore to lay eggs on sandy beaches. They lay close to 100 eggs in a nest, but only one or two survive due to predators, including humans, crabs, dogs, gulls, sharks, and fish. Once the hatchlings leave the nest for the open ocean, they never return to land unless they are laying eggs, sick, injured, or wash up on the beach, dead. Mating occurs far offshore and has rarely been witnessed, so it is impossible to even guess the number of males in existence. Females store sperm during the weeks before the nesting season, and they fertilize their clutches of eggs at the time of laying. Incubation time is about 60 days.
- The most significant threat to hawksbill turtles is harvesting for their tortoiseshell, used to make jewelry and other ornaments and decorations. They are often hunted as a food source. Polluted oceans, loss of nesting beaches, and poaching of eggs contribute to decreased populations. They are dependent on coral reefs, so the improved health of at-risk reefs is critical.
- Education of residents of and visitors to nesting beach communities would help turtle conservation. We can all work to eliminate the use of plastic bags; turtles mistakenly swallow them, thinking they are jellyfish. Beach cleanups and elimination of bright beachfront lighting would assist hatchlings in reaching the ocean.

Teresa Korpal Weyand, Alameda, California

- *Cephalorhynchus hectori*
- Chordata/Mammalia
- Endangered: population trend decreasing
- Roughly the size of a man, these are the smallest dolphins and can be identified by a rounded dorsal fin.
- They live in shallow waters along the New Zealand coast.

- Population is declining because they become entangled in gill nets and trawl nets. Because they swim in shallow water, they are frequently killed by boats. Coastal pollution and construction contribute to their demise.
- The most obvious solution is to ban the use of trawl nets and to post warnings and enforce speed limits for boats.

HINE'S EMERALD DRAGONFLY

Meena Schaldenbrand, Plymouth, Michigan

- *Somatochlora hineana*
- Arthropoda/Insecta
- Listed as Near Threatened by IUCN Red List, and USFWS classifies this insect as Endangered; population trend is stable.
- This flying insect has a metallic-green body, bright-green eyes, and yellow stripes. It is 2 to 5 inches long, and the wingspan is around 3 inches. They prefer to inhabit bogs and low-lying fen meadows (this is a rare type of wetland).
- Found in Wisconsin, Michigan, Illinois, and Missouri
- The species is decreasing due to habitat destruction; wetlands are being drained to create urban areas.
- To recover the species, habitat protection is necessary. Contamination of wetlands by pesticides, including lawn chemicals, should be curtailed.

HIPPOPOTAMUS

Rosanne F. Williamson, Warrenton, Virginia

- *Hippopotamus amphibius*
- Chordata/Mammalia
- Vulnerable: population trend stable
- Purplish and brown in color, the bodies of hippos are covered with sparse hair. They weigh up to 3 tons, are up to 13 feet long, and are around 5 feet tall. Don't be fooled; as large as they are, they are capable of moving quickly on land and in water. They are semiaquatic; they stay cool and sleep in shallow water or on muddy banks in social groups. The water where they nap during their lazy days needs to be deep enough for the animal to completely submerge. At dusk, they feed on grass and plants on land; most of their activity occurs at night. They eat up to 90 pounds of food per night. Their jaws can open up to 150 degrees, and their mouths contain enormous sharp teeth, up to 20 inches long and tusks. Highly territorial, they communicate threats by dung showering and vocalization, consisting of wheezing and honking noises. Predators include humans, lions, and crocodiles. A superpower is that their honking can be up to 115 decibels, a sound that is the equivalent to the noise of loud thunder. Their life span is 50 years.
- Hippos are found in rivers and savannas of the Ethiopian region of central Africa, including 29 different countries.
- They are at risk due to habitat loss and illegal and unregulated hunting for meat and ivory.
- Many protected areas have been established in a number of countries in Africa. Enforcement of this protection is often inadequate.

Serena Brown, Stafford, Virginia

- *Amazilla luciae*
- Chordata/Aves
- Endangered: population trend decreasing
- This species is a medium-sized hummingbird noted for its blue throat and upper chest, bronze tail, and metallic-green upper-body parts.
- They are located in the Agua Valley in north-central Honduras, where their habitat is open canopy thorn forest and scrub areas. Most of them live in the Honduran Emerald Reserve.
- They are endangered because most of their territory has been lost to agriculture and development.
- New conservation initiatives, including reserves, are needed to protect the newfound sites of these birds.

Donna DeSoto, Fairfax, Virginia

- *Camellia hongkongensis*
- Plantae/Theaceae family
- Endangered
- This ornamental tree grows up to 32 feet tall. It has leathery, glossy, oblong leaves that are around 5 inches long, and the leaves grow on reddish-brown-colored branches. The red blossoms have petals that are just under 2 inches each. They bloom from December through February.

- Their usual habitat is in sparse forests in Hong Kong and in other coastal islands of China.
- Threats include urbanization and destruction by fruit tree plantations and logging.
- Efforts to save this plant include protection under forestry regulations, active propagation and subsequent reintroduction into the wild, seed collection, and seedling care.

HONOHONO

Crystal Rousseau, Stafford, Virginia

- *Haplostachys haplostachya*
- Plantae/Lamiaceae family
- Not evaluated by IUCN Red List but classified Critically Imperiled by NatureServe
- This is a perennial shrub in the mint family. It is usually 2 to 3 feet tall but can grow to 5 feet. The leaves are long, soft, and heart shaped. Tiny fragrant white flowers grow on a spike from the center of the plant.

- Endemic to the Big Island of Hawaii
- Species is imperiled because of deforestation, destruction of habitat by feral pigs, and invasion by nonnative plant species.
- Unspecified recovery plans are in progress.

INDIANA BAT

Elly Dyson, Annandale, Virginia

- *Myotis sodalist*
- Chordata/Mammalia
- Listed as Endangered under the current Endangered Species Act of 1973, by USFWS
- These bats have black to chestnut hair, with light-gray to cinnamon-colored hair on their belly, and pink lips. They live in colonies and hibernate in limestone caves during the winter months. Their bodies are less than 4 inches, and they weigh about 0.25 ounce. They live on a diet of insects, including moths, bees, wasps, and mosquitoes.
- They live in forests, crop fields, and grasslands in the eastern United States.
- Their population is at risk due to white-nose syndrome, killing by humans, wind turbines, pesticide use, cave gates, agricultural development, and climate change.
- Ultraviolet rays are being tested and experimented with to try to end white-nose syndrome.

JAGUAR

Barbara Dahlberg, Crofton, Maryland

- *Panthera onca*
- Chordata/Mammalia
- Near Threatened; designated Endangered by USFWS: population trend decreasing
- These are the largest cats in the Americas. Spotted carnivores, they weigh 100 to 250 pounds and live 12 to 15 years.
- They are becoming endangered because they are hunted by farmers who try to prevent them from killing livestock. In addition, their habitat is in jeopardy.
- They live in forests and wetlands in remote regions of Central and South America.
- Their habitats need to be protected, and they could use help to increase breeding. Support the jaguar recovery efforts of the USFWS to try to bring them back into the US.

JELLYFISH TREE

Brenda Page, Herndon, Virginia

- *Medusagyne oppositifolia*
- Plantae/Medusagynaceae family
- Critically Endangered: population decreasing
- This tree grows to a height of 33 feet and has dark, fissured bark and a dense crown of foliage. Leathery leaves have a slightly scalloped edge and turn bright red with age. Small white flowers have numerous stamens and resemble the "head of Medusa" from Greek mythology, which explains the scientific name. The flowers are difficult to see. As round, green fruits dry to maturity, they turn reddish brown and look like larval jellyfish, which is where the common name comes from. After the fruits dry, seeds are exposed and distributed by the wind.
- Located on Mahe Island in the Seychelles, in scrubland on granite slopes
- They are becoming extinct because seeds are unable to germinate due to loss of habitat.
- Protect the trees by law. The trees that grow in the Morne Seychellois National Park are not currently legally protected. Propagation programs are in place in Kew Royal Botanic Gardens and at the Biodiversity Center in Mahe.

Biodiversity and the Firecrown

Peter Hodum

Approximately 400 miles off the coast of central Chile, surrounded by deep ocean for as far as the eye can see from its volcanic ridges and peaks, lie the Juan Fernández Islands. The islands emerged from the ocean as the exposed summits of massive underwater volcanoes several million years ago. Since then, they have served as a refuge for species that arrived on their shores as wanderers, explorers, castaways and refugees. Like on many remote oceanic islands, over time, populations adapted to the different conditions of the islands and evolved into new species, creating unique communities and ecosystems. In the Juan Fernández Islands, these evolutionary processes have led to one of the highest densities of endemic species, those occurring only in a certain area, per unit area of anywhere on the planet. It was that endemism, particularly of the birds of the archipelago, and the threats to its persistence, that initially drew me to the islands nearly 20 years ago. These islands are highly compelling to me, as a conservation biologist. The Juan Fernández Islands are a globally significant biodiversity jewel, yet the existence of many of the archipelago's unique species is under significant threat.

I arrived in the islands for the first time in 1999, having recently completed my PhD in ecology, with the intention of assessing whether or not there might be opportunities to develop a conservation research program focused on the threatened seabird community of the islands. That initial visit provided me the perspective to begin to develop the long-term conservation program that I have helped lead in the islands since 2001. Although our initial focus was on the poorly studied community of seabirds breeding on the islands, of which four of the six species are globally listed by the IUCN as Vulnerable, we quickly realized that there were additional conservation priorities that were not being addressed. As a result, our conservation program, carried out by the conservation nonprofit I work with, Oikonos Ecosystem Knowledge (www.oikonos.org), and as part of my responsibilities at my job at the university, expanded in scope. Our long-term program is dedicated to conducting applied ecological research to inform conservation planning, carrying out conservation actions for priority endangered species, restoring critical native habitat, and working closely through community-based conservation programs.

One of the priority species for us is an iconic emblem of the islands, the Juan Fernández firecrown. This stunning hummingbird, portrayed so beautifully by Sue Bynum in her quilt featured in this book, is endemic to a single island in the world, Robinson Crusoe Island in the Juan Fernández Archipelago. It is critically endangered with extinction, primarily due to loss of native forest habitat and the impacts of invasive plant and animal species.

The firecrown, so named because of the spectacular iridescent golden-ruby feathers on its crown, depends heavily on native forest for its survival. However, only a small fraction of that critical habitat still exists. Even what remains is at risk due to the impacts of introduced plant and animal species. We have been working for more than a decade, in active collaboration with the local community and the national park that composes most of the archipelago, to restore critical habitat and control invasive species. But the scale of our work is insufficient and needs to be increased if future generations of Juan Fernández Islanders are to be able to continue to share their island home with this magical hummingbird.

In addition to our commitment to the firecrown, we are leading efforts to conserve the Másafuera rayadito (*Aphrastura masafuerae*), another critically endangered land bird that is endemic to a single island in the archipelago, and the previously mentioned threatened seabird community. Spending time with the rayadito and two endemic petrel species, Juan Fernández and Stejneger's (*Pterodroma externa* and *Pterodroma longirostris*, respectively), in their cloud-shrouded mountainous habitat on the island of Alejandro Selkirk, amid tree ferns and endemic tree species, has been transformative and inspiring for me. It is a challenging place to work. Even in midsummer, the weather is frequently wet, cold, and windy, and it can feel like you are living inside a cloud for days at a time. But to be confronted by a curious rayadito checking out who or what has entered its mountainous territory or to sit on a high ridge in a petrel colony at night surrounded by a symphony of birds calling in flight, ghosting past gracefully as silhouettes on the wind, are experiences that inspire my work. Our world would be poorer if such natural spectacles disappear.

The conservation work that I have been involved with serves as a case study of the issues confronting the conservation of biodiversity globally. Although much has been written about the growing biodiversity crisis and the accelerating rate of extinction globally, actions to date have been entirely insufficient to address the magnitude of the issue. Nearly one-third of all known species of vertebrates are declining in population size, range, or both. More than 40 percent of all amphibian species and 25 percent of all mammals are globally listed as threatened or endangered. One in eight bird species is in danger of extinction, with 40 percent of the 10,000+ species of birds in the world declining significantly.

For virtually all of these declining species, the principal driving forces are human caused, with habitat loss and alteration, invasive species, direct exploitation (hunting, harvesting, trapping), and climate change being the most globally pervasive human impacts on biodiversity. While the numbers and trends do not make for uplifting reading, the fact that the causes of endangerment for most species are almost invariably of human origin means that we have the capacity to work to reverse them if the will and commitment exist.

Science alone is insufficient to advance lasting conservation. Information in and of itself does not necessarily lead to caring or support, themselves necessary for action to be taken and sustained.

Ultimately, conservation of endangered species and ecosystems is a human issue. For long-term conservation to be effective and successful, societal values and priorities need to change. To accomplish this, we need not only to reach people but also to touch them. And that is where creative and genuine engagement is so essential. Local communities have to be involved actively and substantively in conservation efforts. There has to be a genuine commitment to the community, not just to the conservation outcome. Over time, that commitment to and involvement of the community builds the trust and credibility necessary for long-term solutions to be developed.

Conservation solutions come from different disciplines and different ways of knowing with communities.

And this is where we need to return to the idea of creative engagement. Through artistic, educational, social, and technical training activities and programs, community members can access and share in the ownership of the process. These approaches are essential complements to the science of conservation in advancing solutions that will be long lasting.

This is the approach that we have taken in Chile. We actively collaborate with experts in the creative use of different artistic media, including painting, creative writing, sewing of stuffed animals, and performance art to engage people in local communities. In addition, our team in the islands comprises island residents whom we have trained, and now carry out our program—conservation leaders in their own community. And we create opportunities for local residents to engage through artistic workshops, educational talks, and volunteer activities such as the removal of invasive plants from critical Juan Fernández firecrown habitat.

This book is an inspiring and powerful example of how thoughtful art can communicate conservation messages in an accessible and meaningful way. Each quilt tells a story through its imagery and touches us in a way that a graph or a series of numbers does not. I consider such creative efforts to be vital complements to science in our efforts to conserve biodiversity globally.

We all can play a role in biodiversity conservation. It is an exciting time, since there has never been a greater range of options for involvement. Volunteer with a community citizen science project, the results of which frequently are used in conservation planning. Help out with local habitat restoration projects. An activity as simple as getting together with other community members to remove invasive plants from a local park or to plant native species can improve habitat quality as well as the aesthetics of the area. Donate to organizations, whether local grassroots or larger international, that address conservation issues important to you. Write to elected officials to communicate your position on issues. But make your voice heard, because the fates of magical species such as the firecrown rest in our collective hands.

Peter Hodum
Associate professor, Biology Department and Environmental Policy and Decision Making Program, University of Puget Sound
June 26, 2018

Susan M. Bynum, Falls Church, Virginia

- *Sephanoides fernandensis*
- Chordata/Aves
- Critically Endangered: population trend decreasing
- This little hummingbird is around 4.5 inches. Males are bright orange or cinnamon colored with an iridescent gold crown. The female is a little smaller, has a white underside, and is greenish blue with an iridescent blue crown. The male and female look so different that they were once thought to be two entirely different species. They feed on nectar from a variety of plants and sometimes eat insects.
- They live only on Robinson Crusoe Island in the Juan Fernández Archipelago.
- The population decline is blamed on habitat destruction by humans and degradation due to encroachment by nonnative animals such as rabbits and goats. Predatory animals that have been introduced to the island and pose threats include cats, rats, mice, and coatis. Invasion of nonnative plants threatens the native plants this hummingbird uses for nesting and feeding. In 2010 a devastating tsunami occurred, which had a significant impact on the bird's population.
- Conservation efforts include habitat restoration in the Plazoleta del Yunque study area, population monitoring, the creation of a citizen science program to complement the population monitoring, and the establishment of a regular program of cat control, in cooperation with residents.

Jason and Karen Wolfson, Chantilly, Virginia

KAKAPO

- *Strigops habroptila*
- Chordata/Aves
- Critically Endangered: population increasing
- This is a large solitary bird, ranging from 6 to 7 pounds and 23 to 25 inches long. Moss green with yellow and black-splotched feathers perfect for camouflage, it is the only parrot in the world that can't fly. It is both herbivorous and nocturnal; although it lives on the ground, it is a great climber, using the wings for balance and to "parachute" down to the ground. They live an average of 58 years, but one is known to have lived for 120 years. They have an amusing collection of vocalizations that can be heard on the internet. A superpower they have is the sounds they make. One almost sounds like the noise of a tuba; another is like the loud croaking of a frog. Their sounds can travel more than 3 miles, which attract predators including weasels, ferrets, stoats, rats, cats, and dogs.
- Found only in New Zealand
- The reason that populations have declined is that predators were introduced by humans, and there is low fertility.
- There is a kakapo recovery program. To revive the species, remove predators from island habitats and relocate the kakapo to safe, monitored habitats. Close monitoring of all kakapo would be beneficial.

Karner Blue Butterfly

Nancy Karst, Springfield, Virginia

- *Lycaeidas (Plebejus) melissa samuelis*
- Arthropoda/Insecta
- Not evaluated by IUCN Red List but listed as Vulnerable by NatureServe
- These tiny butterflies have a wingspan of 1 inch. They love open, sunny areas in oak savannas and pine barrens. They are dependent on wild blue lupines for food.
- They are found in the Great Lakes states: Wisconsin, Indiana, Minnesota, Michigan, and New York.
- They are at risk because their habitat, where the blue lupines grow, is being lost to development. Their predators are spiders and other insects, deer, and birds.
- Naturalists are attempting habitat conservation programs as well as propagation of the species and releasing them to more-favorable habitats. Large areas of blue lupines are being replanted.

Miki Willa, Spokane, Washington

- *Hibiscus waimeae*
- Plantae/Malvaceae family
- Not evaluated by IUCN Red List but designated Imperiled by NatureServe
- This large shrub is 6 to 15 feet tall, and up to 14 feet wide. The medium-green leaves are 2 to 10 inches long, and the plant tolerates both dry and moist conditions. Blooms, which last only one day, are smaller than most hibiscus flowers and are white, with red stamens; this is the only fragrant hibiscus.

- Endemic to the Hawaiian island of Kaua'i.
- These plants hybridize readily, and they are in danger due to cross-pollination with nonnative species.
- Careful hand pollination and isolation will allow for collection and storage of seeds for future planting and perpetuation of this species.

KILLER WHALE

Anna Willard, Oak Hill, Virginia

- *Orcinus orca*
- Chordata/Mammalia
- Listed as "data deficient" by the IUCN Red List; designated Endangered by the US Endangered Species Act and by the Canadian Species at Risk Act
- This animal is part of the dolphin family and has distinctive black-and-white markings. They are 22 to 33 feet long and can weigh up to 6 tons. These social animals hunt in pods, eating fish, seals, sea lions, dolphins, sharks, squid, octopus, turtles, birds, otters, and even other whales; they consume an average of 100 pounds of food a day. At the top of the marine food chain, they play a significant role in the ecosystem. Females live an average of 63 years, and the average life span of males is 36 years. Males and females have multiple mates throughout their lifetime. After mating, males are not involved in rearing their offspring. The mothers teach their young hunting and parenting skills. They use sonar abilities to navigate, and vocalizations aid in communication and migration. A superpower of this species is that specific dialects exist within pods. The fossil history of orcas dates to an epoch five million years ago.
- Located in every ocean but prefers colder water
- They are endangered due to pollution and habitat loss, depletion of prey species, and conflicts with fishing vessels, whaling efforts, and other maritime activities.
- Steps to manage recovery involve overharvesting of prey species and habitat conservation.

KOMODO DRAGON

Joanne Strehle Bast, Littlestown, Pennsylvania

- *Varanus komodoensis*
- Chordata/Reptilia
- Vulnerable
- These enormous monitor lizards are strong, stealthy, and patient hunters. This is the largest, heaviest lizard in the world, which grows up to 10 feet long and can weigh more than 300 pounds; a more typical weight is 150 pounds. Stone colored, containing large scales and a yellow forked tongue, they have large, muscular tails. A superpower is that they are able to consume 80 percent of their own body weight in a single meal. Keen vision allows them to see things almost a thousand feet away, and they have a keen sense of smell. They will eat practically anything, including smaller komodo dragons, water buffalo, and even humans.
- They are located in tropical savanna forests and are in beaches to ridgetops in the Lesser Sunda islands of Indonesia, including Komodo Island.

- They are at risk because poachers hunt them and encroach on them. They are affected by natural disasters, and the number of egg-laying females is in decline.
- Establishment of Komodo National Park has helped protect the dragons from various threats. The Komodo Survival Program assists in community awareness, instructing the locals about preserving land and training individuals who work with these animals to not harm them while staying safe themselves. Preservation requires prevention of overhunting deer, slash-and-burn agriculture, and competition for resources with feral dogs that were introduced by people. There has been some breeding success at the National and the Cincinnati Zoos.

Bobbie Dewees, Springfield, Virginia

- *Telmatobius culeus*
- Chordata/Amphibia
- Critically Endangered: population decreasing
- This is one of the world's largest aquatic frogs, sometimes measuring 20 inches, outstretched. They spend their entire lives in fresh water. Their wrinkly skin has adapted to absorb oxygen at the high altitudes where they live.
- They are endemic to Lake Titicaca, on the border of Peru and Bolivia in South America.
- At risk due to overcollection for human consumption and medicinal purposes, pollution from illegal heavy-metal mining, and human waste. Invasive species are taking over their habitat.
- Aquatic habitat conditions need to be improved so they will have a suitable environment. Steps toward revival could include captive breeding programs, which have been unsuccessful so far. Laws should exist to make collection illegal.

LESSER CHAMELEON

Donna DeSoto, Fairfax, Virginia

- *Furcifer minor*
- Chordata/Reptilia
- Endangered: population decreasing
- This terrestrial reptile is diurnal and enjoys a solitary lifestyle; in fact, they are often aggressive toward their own species. They are 6 to 10 inches long, and the female is the more colorful. They are mostly yellow and bright green, with yellow, blue, violet, and orange markings. Females lay four to 16 eggs up to three times a year. These are hunters who patiently wait for insects and invertebrates before shooting out a long, sticky tongue to capture their victim. Their color can change rapidly.

- Lives only in the central highlands of Madagascar
- As the native tapia forest habitat disappears due to tourmaline and quartz mining and logging, the chameleons are being displaced and are found in locations that put them in danger: coffee plantations, villages, and orchards. They are exported for the pet market.
- Conservation efforts include banning their exportation, restricting trade and monitoring collection, and establishing and protecting safe areas for them to live.

Karin Täuber, Blacksburg, Virginia

LOGGERHEAD TURTLE

- *Caretta caretta*
- Chordata/Reptilia
- Vulnerable: population trend decreasing
- This turtle weighs 155 to 375 pounds and has a slightly heart-shaped shell between 2.5 and 3.5 feet long. Reddish brown in color, it has a large head and strong jaw muscles to enable it to crush and eat shellfish. Mature females travel thousands of miles to return to the same general area where they hatched as babies to lay their own eggs. Turtles nest every two or three years, emerging onto the beach and laying an average of four clutches of 100 to 126 eggs. The nesting season begins in April and ends in September. They can live for 50 years and longer.
- They are widely distributed mostly in subtropical and temperate regions and are found on beaches, in water, and in coastal areas. They travel long distances, following major warm ocean currents.
- Threats include loss or degradation of nesting habitat due to coastal development, the disorientation of hatchlings by beachfront lighting, nest disturbance by predators, degradation of foraging habitat, marine pollution and debris, water-craft strikes, disease, and incidental take from channel dredging and commercial fishing. There is particular concern about the extensive incidental take of juvenile loggerheads in the eastern Atlantic. Directed harvest for loggerheads still occurs in many places (particularly in the Bahamas, Cuba, and Mexico) and is a serious threat to loggerhead recovery.
- Conservation efforts in one country may be jeopardized by activities in another. The federal agencies NMFS and USFWS issued regulations to eliminate or reduce threats, but protecting sea turtles on US nesting beaches and in US waters alone is not sufficient to ensure the continued existence of the species. In the south-eastern US, significant nest protection efforts and beach habitat protection are underway for most nesting areas, and progress has been made to reduce mortality from commercial fisheries in US waters with the enforcement of turtle-excluder-device regulations. Many coastal areas in Florida, Georgia, and South Carolina have developed lighting ordinances to reduce hatchling disorientations. US nesting beaches have been acquired for long-term protection. The migratory nature of loggerheads severely compromises these efforts once the turtles move outside US waters, however.

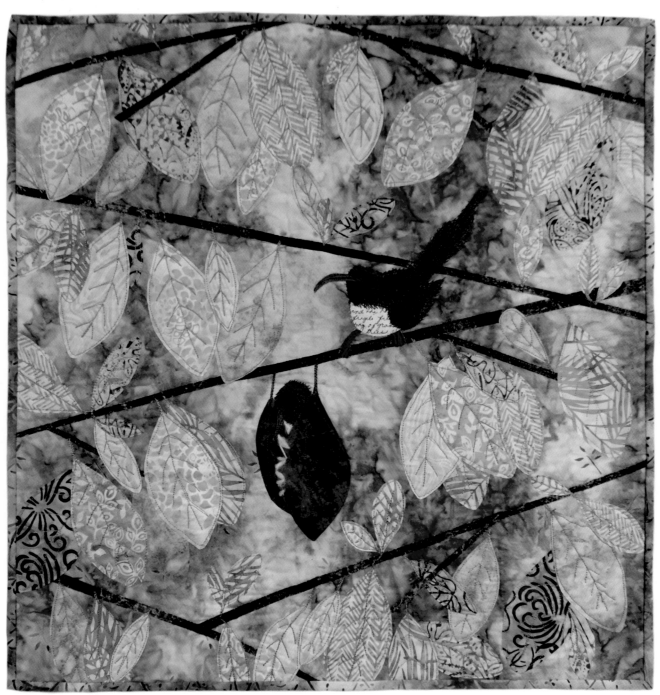

Sue Graham, Ashburn, Virginia

LONG-BILLED TAILORBIRD

- *Artisornis sousae* (also commonly known as Mozambique forest-warbler)
- Chordata/Aves
- Endangered: population trend stable
- This is a small warbler that has both a long beak and a long tail. Feathers are grayish, and the bird is brown on the face and head. These birds prefer the forest canopy; they are territorial and eat invertebrates. The male and female are similar in appearance.
- Found in two forests: the East Usambara Mountains in northeastern Tanzania, and in the Njesi Plateau in northern Mozambique, and in at least two protected areas: the Amani Nature Reserve, which has an active conservation program, and the Nilo Nature Reserve.
- They are in danger because of forest destruction from mining, pole cutting, cultivation, and firewood collection. This habitat degradation continues even within forest reserves. The removal of vegetation bordering tea plantations, including lantana bushes, may cause their habitat to disappear.
- To revive the species, conservation of the two protected reserve areas is necessary. A population-monitoring program, field surveys, and educational programs are being conducted by the Wildlife Conservation Society of Tanzania.

Eileen Doughty, Vienna, Virginia

LONGLEAF PINE

- *Pinus palustris*
- Plantae/Pinaceae family
- Endangered: population decreasing
- These coniferous evergreens grow 98 to 115 feet tall and are just over 2 feet in diameter. The needles average 12 inches long, and the cones average 8 inches in length. They require a damp, warm climate and moist soil. They live to be more than 500 years old, and they are especially sought after as timber because the high-quality wood is both straight and strong. Turpentine is one of the products that come from chipped wood. To learn more about these trees, check out this eight-minute video online: http://longleafpine.org/.
- Located in the southeastern US, from Virginia to East Texas to the Gulf of Mexico coastal plains.
- They are at risk because of logging and loss of habitat from land that has been converted to farmland and pastures.
- In attempts to conserve this species, there are a number of protected areas where controlled burning occurs, which is beneficial to seedlings and the growth of these trees. The number of reserves should be increased for greater genetic diversity.

Teresa Korpal Weyand, Alameda, California

- *Dryococelus australis* (also commonly known as a tree lobster)
- Arthropoda/Insecta
- Critically Endangered
- This blackish-brown insect has six legs and is approximately 6 inches long. They have a lobsterlike exoskeleton and live in tea trees. They are active at night, are without wings, and feed on only one species of shrub.
- They once were endemic to Lord Howe Island, on the east coast of Australia, but were declared endangered when nonnative rats destroyed them. They have since been discovered on a small nearby volcanic rock island called Balls Pyramid.
- They are at risk because the remaining population is very small. Any change to the small island where they exist, such as the introduction of black rats or other nonnative vermin, loss of the vegetation they feed on, or poaching, could be catastrophic to the species.
- To preserve the species, rats need to be eradicated from Lord Howe Island and prevented from infesting Balls Pyramid. Captive breeding could allow for reintroduction and subsequent breeding within the wild population. Encourage community awareness about this insect and prevent poaching.

MALAYAN TAPIR

Dianne Mehlinger, Arlington, Virginia

- *Tapirus indictus*
- Chordata/Mammalia
- Endangered: population trend decreasing
- Tapirs are large, pig-shaped mammals. Their super-power is a prehensile nose used for grabbing food and for snorkeling underwater. They eat fruits and leaves, are solitary, and are mostly nocturnal. This animal is the largest variety of tapir, weighing 500 to 800 pounds and growing up to 6 feet long. They stand 29 to 42 inches, shoulder height. Extraordinarily, this mammal has existed since the Eocene epoch, 56 to 33.9 million years ago.

- They are native to Indonesia, Malaysia, Myanmar, and Thailand.
- The species is endangered because deforestation has led to a loss of habitat. Hunting and road killing present other hazards.
- Steps to revive the species could include conserving habitats, fostering genetic diversity, research, public awareness and education, and government action.

Eileen Thomas, Bristow, Virginia

MANDRILL

- *Mandrillus sphinx*
- Chordata/Mammalia
- Vulnerable
- This animal is just over 20 inches tall and weighs approximately 70 pounds. They have long, powerful arms and legs and a big head. The coloration of the body is olive green, with a brilliant bluish/purplish rump. Striking in appearance, the face has a bright-red stripe down the middle, and the sides of the snout are blue ridged, vertically. Red fur patches are above the eyes, and they have an orange/yellow beard. Their diet is fruits, roots, insects, and small fish and reptiles. Life span is 46 years.
- Found in tropical rainforests of Equatorial Africa, from the Sanaga River to the Congo River.
- Species is vulnerable because of deforestation, caused mostly by building new roads and human settlement. They are hunted for their meat.
- There are several reserves, including Lope National Park in Gabon. They are listed and somewhat protected by CITES, but much needs to be done to protect their habitat from logging and to prevent hunting.

Karen Troutman, Alexandria, Virginia

- *Chrysocyon brachyurus*
- Chordata/Mammalia
- Near Threatened: listed as Vulnerable in parts of South America
- According to the Smithsonian National Zoo and Conservation Biology Institute, this animal "looks like a fox, is called a wolf, and is closely related to neither." Their fur is reddish brown to golden orange, but the most distinctive part of their appearance is long black legs, good for digging and leaping, and a black mane. They are 3 feet tall, weigh 51 pounds, and have a long tail and large, 7-inch ears. A superpower they have is that they are able to rotate their ears so they can listen for animals in the grass. They don't travel in packs, or howl, but make loud barking or roaring sounds. They are mostly vegetarians, eating fruit and vegetables, besides small mammals and fish. They are monogamous and patrol an area of 12 square miles with their mates. They mark their territory and thus earned the nickname "skunk wolf." In captivity, they live for up to 15 years; we don't know how long they live in the wild.
- Maned wolves are located in Argentina, Bolivia, Brazil, Paraguay, and Uruguay, in rainforests and savannas.
- They are at risk because of loss of habitat and deforestation, as well as diseases from contact with domestic animals, and they are often hit by cars. They are killed by men who wrongly believe they are a danger to people and livestock.
- Many parts of their range protect them, and hunting is prohibited. Public awareness is necessary to increase tolerance toward the species. Domestic dogs need to be vaccinated to prevent the spread of disease. The Brazilian and Argentinian governments have drawn up plans for conservation.

MARKHOR

Pam Shanley, Summerville, South Carolina

- *Capra falconeri*
- Chordata/Mammalia
- Near Threatened: population trend increasing; this subspecies is designated Endangered by CITES.
- Largest of the goat family, and therefore adept climbers, this animal's corkscrew-like, spiraled horns can be up to 5 feet long. Their fur is reddish gray to gray, and the length of the fur varies according to the season. Their average weight is 90 to 240 pounds, they are 37 to 40 inches tall at their shoulders, and their life span is around 12 or 13 years. They are diurnal (active in the daytime) and graze on grass and leaves eight to 12 hours a day. They are preyed upon by snow leopards, wolves, lynxes, and humans.
- Habitat is northern Pakistan, central Asia, and India, in the Himalayan mountain range.
- This species is in trouble because they are hunted for trophies, and the horns are sold in the Asian medicine market. Human settlement jeopardizes populations.
- Although they are Pakistan's national animal, hunting continues and ought to be curtailed. There are sanctuaries in Jammu and Kashmir, a state in northern India. These animals reside in zoos in Los Angeles and New York. A controversial Trophy Hunting Program is being considered, but it is unknown whether this practice will actually aid the effort to revive the species.

MENZIES' WALLFLOWER

Katherine Heslep, Alexandria, Virginia

- *Erysimum menziesii*
- Plantae/Brassicaceae family
- Not evaluated by the IUCN; listed as Imperiled by NatureServe
- This wallflower is a low-growing biennial in the mustard family. It has a rosette of fleshy, succulent-type leaves, and it blooms from February to April.
- Found in gravelly substrate in three counties in California: Humboldt, Mendocino, and Monterey.
- They are imperiled because of deer predation, sand mining, the impact of recreational use of the habitat by humans, and crowding by invasive species such as ice plants.
- Removal of invasive species and then replanting them has helped restoration efforts to increase the population in one county. There is a lack of method implemented to monitor the restoration efforts on a routine basis, and there is no dedicated source of funding, so more work needs to be done.

Dottie Dane, Annandale, Virginia

- *Erythronium propullans*
- Plantae/Liliaceae family
- Not evaluated by the IUCN Red List, this species is classified as Endangered by the USFWS.
- This is a spring-blooming plant with a flower no larger than 1 inch. It grows and flowers before the leaves come out on deciduous trees in mostly maple and basswood forests, and on some floodplains along with elms and cottonwood trees. It is found among the leaves on the moist forest floor, blooming with other ephemerals such as spring beauty and Dutchman's breeches. "Erythronium" comes from the Greek word meaning red, referring to the mottled spots on the green leaves, which look like a trout. Incidentally, the plant blooms during trout-fishing season.
- The only places in the world where this plant grows are in three counties in southeastern Minnesota, south of the Twin Cities and along the Cannon River, and there is one small colony at the Minnesota Landscape Arboretum.
- These little lilies occur in a very small range. They cannot adapt to the threats of farming, cattle grazing, logging, housing developments, or recreational use of the land by humans walking or vehicles that compact the soil.
- Most of the habitat is preserved by parks and private preserves, such as the Nature Conservancy. There is a voluntary program of farmers in a private registry. There is no manipulation of the vegetation. Retaining walls are being constructed on Prairie Creek at Big Woods State Park near Nerstrand, and conservationists are working on shoreline stabilization along the Cannon River to minimize erosion from flash floods.

MITCHELL'S SATYR BUTTERFLY

Susan J. Sladek, Fairfax, Virginia

- *Neonympha mitchellii mitchellii*
- Arthropoda/Insecta
- Not evaluated by the IUCN Red List, classified as Imperiled by NatureServe, and as Endangered by USFWS
- This butterfly is mostly brown with some orange and silver markings and is just under 2 inches. As caterpillars, they eat grassy plants, but adults are said not to eat or drink anything; their life span is two weeks.
- They live in Michigan and possibly Indiana. They spend their entire short life near their place of birth, at the woodland edge of a prairie fen.

- Primarily at risk because their habitat is being lost due to pesticides and pollutants. They are prized by butterfly collectors.
- It is illegal to collect them without a permit from the USFWS. Michigan, under a federal grant, has worked with Indiana to develop a recovery plan both for this butterfly and for prairie fens. Extensive plans call for building awareness, protecting and restoring fens, and providing maintenance guidelines. The Toledo Zoo has attempted restoration of the species in captivity. Conservationists are working to educate the public about this little species and to protect their habitat.

Dena Gail Brannen, Reston, Virginia

- *Clematis morefieldii* (also known commonly as Huntsville vasevine)
- Plantae/Ranunculacea family
- Not evaluated on the IUCN Red List but listed as Imperiled by NatureServe
- This is a flowering perennial vine in the buttercup family.
- Located in two counties in Alabama and Tennessee, this plant grows in rocky limestone woods in patches near springs. It grows on south- and southwest-facing slopes at elevations of 800 to 1,100 feet.

- Their major threat is residential development. They are possibly at risk in Tennessee due to quarrying.
- The plants need protection from residential development. Research could determine how the plant responds to gaps in the forest canopy. More information is required about germination and reproduction. Additional surveys in areas surrounding current populations would be useful.

Sarah Lykins Entsminger, Ashburn, Virginia

Mountain Sweet Pitcher Plant

- *Sarracenia rubra* subsp. *jonesii*
- Plantae/Sarraceniaceae family
- Not evaluated by IUCN; Endangered according to USFWS and ESA
- This species is a carnivorous perennial herb, growing from 21 to 73 inches tall in clusters in mountain bogs. The tall, hollow, pitcher-shaped leaves are filled with a sweet-smelling liquid. Insects fall through the slippery smooth opening into a tube, which is filled with downward-pointing hairs that keep the insects captive. The plant secretes a fluid containing enzymes that digest the insect. Those nutrients are then incorporated into the plant's tissues. Scientists believe that the absorption of minerals from insects allows the plant to survive in habitats of nutrient-poor soils. Flowers appear from April to June, and the leaves have red veins on bright-green coppery backgrounds. Blooms and leaves appear red and yellow; the plants die off by the first frost.
- They grow in the foothills of the Blue Ridge Mountains in upstate South Carolina and southwestern North Carolina.
- The most serious threat to these plants is destruction and degradation of its wetland bog habitat. Overcollection by amateur plant collectors and professional botanists who are interested in carnivorous plants is another threat.
- Protect existing populations, reestablish nursery-bred plants into their historical habitat, develop cultivated sources of the plant for long-term seed storage and rhizomes, and enforce laws to protect the species.

Laura Robertson, Kearneysville, West Virginia

- *Rana muscosa*
- Chordata/Amphibia
- Endangered: population decreasing
- These medium-sized frogs, up to 3.5 inches long, are mostly brownish yellow, with markings that resemble lichen. They live in lakes, rivers, streams, and ponds. They prey on various bugs and catch them with their long, sticky tongues. A superpower is that when they sense they are in danger, they produce a garlicky scent as a defense mechanism.
- Their range is the Sierra Nevada of California.
- The main threat to these amphibians is nonnative fish. They are severely affected by contaminants, livestock, disease, and drought.
- Most remaining frogs live on federally managed, protected land.

Maggie Ward, Warrenton, Virginia

- *Equus zebra*
- Chordata/Mammalia
- Vulnerable
- These stocky herbivores are the smallest of all zebra species. As with all zebras, they have a unique pattern of black-and-white stripes and a white belly. Their manes are short haired and stand straight up, and they have ears that are 8 inches long. They survive for approximately 20 years and live in herds. They are excellent climbers, are known to dig for water, and enjoy a daily dust bath.

- They live in the mountainous and plateau regions of South Africa, primarily in national park reserves.
- They face the loss of their habitat to growing agricultural needs. They compete for food with domestic livestock and are at risk due to poaching and hunting, mostly for their pelts. Cross-species interbreeding is of concern.
- The South African government has established the Mountain Zebra National Park. This species is legally protected from hunters.

NELLIE CORY DWARF CACTUS

Suzanne Meader, Sterling, Virginia

- *Escobaria minima*
- Plantae/Cactaceae family
- Although designated by IUCN Red List as of least concern, this species is listed as federally Endangered by USFWS: the population is stable.
- This tiny succulent perennial grows to 1.5 inches tall. Most cacti have needlelike spines; this one has short, blunt, peg-like spines. They are so numerous and close together that the stem is completely hidden. Bright pink flowers appear March through June. Seeds are dark brown or black and egg shaped.

- Found in a particular area of Brewster County, West Texas, in the Chihuahuan Desert scrub.
- A threat is the illegal collection at roadsides.
- Anticollection laws should be enforced, and a population study needs to be conducted.

Barbara Wise, Reston, Virginia

- *Scirpus ancistrochaetus*
- Plantae/Cyperaceae family
- Near Threatened: population decreasing
- This plant grows 30 to 70 inches tall. From June through July, stems of drooping flower heads appear with brown-colored clusters of flowers. The plant has narrow leaves, and it is difficult to locate and recognize.
- Found in the Appalachian range from Vermont and New Hampshire to western Virginia, in wetlands, seasonal pools, small ponds, and shallow sinkholes.

- This plant is affected by changes in the hydrology of its environment. It suffers from changes occurring as a result of residential and agricultural development, road construction, and quarrying. Dry spells or flooding can dramatically alter the hydrology of the environment and threaten the species.
- The recovery strategy involves protecting existing habitats from deterioration and destruction. Implementing this strategy can be difficult. When the bulrush is located on private land in an area less than an acre, the site may not qualify for the legal protections provided by the Endangered Species Act.

Nicki Allen, Springfield, Virginia

NORTHERN BROWN
KIWI

- *Apteryx mantelli*
- Chordata/Aves
- Vulnerable: population stable
- This flightless nocturnal bird is 1.5 to 2 feet tall. Feathers resemble a shaggy fur overcoat.
- Lives on the North Island of New Zealand
- Predators include dogs, cats, ferrets, and stoats, the last of which are part of the weasel family. Harvesting of native forests has pushed the brown kiwi population closer to humans and its predators.
- Community education has led to programs such as kiwi aversion training for dogs; individuals are becoming "dog control" rangers. In addition, free housing and subdivisions of cats and dogs in vulnerable geographic areas are being established.

Laura Catherine Gilmartin, Stafford, Virginia

- *Lasiorhinus krefftii*
- Chordata/Mammalia
- Critically Endangered: population trend stable
- Weighing up to almost 90 pounds, this is the largest herbivorous burrowing mammal in the world. These strong, chunky animals have a broad head; short, stout legs; and strong claws for digging. They are nocturnal marsupials and subsist on grass. The average life span is 10 to 12 years.
- Endemic to Australia, at Epping Forest National Park and in Richard Underwood Nature Refuge

- Population could be lost because of extensive habitat destruction, competition for food with kangaroos, droughts, wildfires leading to loss of food, and increased susceptibility to disease and inbreeding.
- A dingo-proof fence was built around the wombat habitat at Epping Forest. In addition, the population was split to reduce the risk of losing the species in case of a fire, flood, disease, or significant predation.

Nicki Allen, Springfield, Virginia

- *Strix occidentalis caurina*
- Chordata/Aves
- Near Threatened: population trend decreasing
- A large dark- to chestnut-brown owl, with big, dark eyes. They live in forests 150 to 200 years old, characterized by dense canopy closure of mature and old-growth trees.
- Located in British Columbia, Oregon, Northern California, and Washington State
- Decline in numbers is due to timber harvesting in their habitat, and competition from encroaching barred owls. Barred owls are larger than spotted owls and more aggressive, having a broader diet, which makes them more resilient than spotted owls.
- In 1990, the northern spotted owl was included in the Endangered Species Act. This act paved the way for the Northwest Forest Plan to provide protections for this owl and its habitat. The USFWS is currently studying the effect of removing barred owls from certain areas where spotted owls live. These actions have created controversy because of the killing of a common species to potentially benefit a rare species.

NORTHERN WHITE RHINOCEROS

Karla Vernon, Vienna, Virginia

- *Ceratotherium simum* subsp. *cottoni*
- Chordata/Mammalia
- Near Threatened; in fact, this subspecies may be newly extinct.
- The third-largest African animal, weighing from 1.6 to 4 tons and measuring 11 to 14 feet. Do you know the color of a northern white rhino? They are actually gray, not white, and are distinguished from black rhinos by the shape of their mouth. These herbivores have a wide, squared mouth and jaw, which allows them to graze efficiently on grass.
- The remaining northern white rhinos, if any are still alive, live on Ol Pejeta Conservancy, located in Kenya. The conservancy is a 700-acre enclosure with around-the-clock armed guards keeping watch and supplying food and companionship.
- Poachers and intense civil war over the years have decimated the population, and they are now believed to be extinct in the wild. In traditional Chinese medicine, the ingestion of powdered rhino horn is used to treat many disorders, even though there are other treatments readily available. The animals have been slaughtered just for their prized horns. The Yemenis traditionally made ceremonial dagger handles with them. The rhino horn is displayed to show a family's wealth and success, worth more than its weight in gold.
- Any remaining animals in captivity are no longer capable of natural reproduction. It is hoped that in vitro fertilization and embryo transfer to a southern white rhino, acting as a surrogate mother, will prolong this species. There are various global funding drives to raise money for the expensive in vitro process and experimentation.

OCELOT

Marisela Rumberg, Annandale, Virginia

- *Leopardus pardalis*
- Chordata/Mammalia
- The IUCN Red List classifies this species as of least concern, with population trends decreasing; USFWS lists the ocelot as Endangered.
- This nocturnal animal, which prefers to sleep in brush and trees, is about twice the size of a house cat. They have a long tail and distinctive blotchy markings on a coat of tawny yellow to reddish gray and white. Carnivores, they eat a varied diet, from frogs and iguanas to rabbits and rodents, monkeys, fish, and birds.

- A broad range includes Arizona and Texas in the US, and in Central and South America, except for Chile. They live in caves, holes inside trees, tropical rainforests, or other large and dense forests.
- The major threat is habitat loss; in the past, they were poached for their fur.
- Protect their habitat, continue the ban on hunting.

Linda M. Moore, Annandale, Virginia

OHLONE TIGER BEETLE

- *Cicindela ohlone*
- Arthropoda/Insecta
- Not evaluated by the IUCN Red List but listed Critically Imperiled by NatureServe
- This small, half-inch bug is a ferocious and agile predator that seizes its prey with sickle-shaped jaws. They are bright green with bronze-colored markings.
- They live in Santa Cruz County, California. Their habitat is clayey soil in grasslands of coastal terrace prairies.
- They are found in areas along the Pacific Ocean, of interest for home development, which has resulted in the destruction of their habitat. Invasive nonnative plant species have caused further damage to their habitat. The population has been adversely affected by pesticide runoff harmful to these insects and by unrestricted collection. The species is prized by insect collectors because of their color.
- These beetles are already protected under the Endangered Species Act, but to restore the species, several actions must be taken; reducing encroachment by nonnative plants with controlled burns, restricting collecting, erecting temporary fences during mating season to block trails from hikers and mountain bikers, redirecting cattle grazing, restricting the use of gravel over trails, and enforcement of conservation efforts.

WHAT ABOUT THE WETLANDS?
John Overland

For as long as I can remember I've been exploring and working in wetlands. As a kid growing up in a small southern Minnesota town we would explore, play, and spend countless hours in the Hanska slough. Frogs, toads, snakes, worms, bugs, and blackbirds were everywhere, and we built numerous forts in and around the slough, with any materials we could scavenge. In my memory it was a huge wetland expanse that went on as far as the eye could see, and undiscovered creatures surely lurked deeper in the cattail jungle. In reality it is much smaller than I recall.

When my family moved to Morris in west-central Minnesota, the Green River (little more than a ditch through town), Pomme de Terre River, and numerous prairie pothole wetlands became my playground. Turtles, crayfish, newts, tadpoles, and carp were added to the list of animals encountered. From there it was off to college in Bemidji, in north-central Minnesota, where the numerous lakes, rivers, and expansive wetlands provided recreation and refuge from higher education. After receiving a degree in biology it was back to the prairie potholes, but this time in the Red River valley and Fargo, North Dakota. There I researched wetland invertebrates and helped others working with waterfowl and blackbirds. With a zoology graduate degree in hand, it was time to find a job and, I hoped, make more than my $375 per month research assistant stipend. Wetland consulting in and around the Twin Cities of Minneapolis and St. Paul was where I landed. After about eight years working for various consulting firms and my own company in central Minnesota, I accepted a wetland position in Brainerd with the state of Minnesota, where I have been for the last 22 years.

Wetlands are a unique part of the landscape. They are transitional between dry upland habitats and open-water lakes and rivers. Because wetlands have characteristics both of upland and aquatic habitats, they are diverse habitats important to numerous plant and animal species, including many endangered species. Wetlands make up a relatively small part of the total landscape, but they provide habitat to approximately half of endangered animals in the US. The transitional nature of wetlands and regulations associated with them make them controversial areas. Few would consider planting agricultural crops or building homes in a lake or river; these things are better suited to dry land. But a wetland's transitional nature between water and dry land means that they are often impacted by development and agriculture.

One of my primary responsibilities was to assist local governments implementing the Minnesota Wetland Conservation Act. The Wetland Conservation Act is similar to, but independent of, federal wetland regulations in the Clean Water Act administered by the US Corps of Engineers. The Wetland Conservation Act is a state law, implemented by local governments (e.g., cities, counties, and watershed districts); my position provided oversight and technical support to the local governments. Along with local government partners I evaluated various development and infrastructure projects to determine if wetland impacts could be avoided or minimized. Wetland impacts that could not be avoided or further minimized typically needed to be replaced with restored or new wetland resources, so the state and federal no-net-loss goal could be realized.

For the last few years I have transitioned to working exclusively with wetland banking. Wetland banking is a process where landowners and entrepreneurs work with ecologists and natural-resource professionals to restore or create new wetland resources and generate wetland mitigation "credits" that are sold to others as replacement for their wetland impacts. Someone establishing a wetland bank is typically motivated both by philosophical and financial objectives, because the wetland credits are sold to offset losses elsewhere. This makes wetland banking different from other restoration and conservation programs, where wetlands are added to the landscape and not directly used to compensate for other wetland losses. While some may see wetland banking as a motivational conflict, I believe that economic gain is too often pitted against altruistic resource protection and restoration. While we all have the best of intentions, economic forces will almost always win over good intentions alone. Even with regulations in place, wetlands are lost due to economic forces, so why not use these same economic forces to restore and permanently protect good-quality wetlands to replace those that are lost?

Conservation banking is a similar system used in many states to protect endangered species and their habitats. Like wetland banks, conservation banks preserve, restore, and permanently protect critical habitats and areas used by endangered species. Once again, economic forces are used to bring together diverse interests and achieve the goal of species and habitat protection. Where there was once only conflict between economic and resource protection interests, there is now a large and expanding business community built around resource protection to satisfy regulatory requirements. This reality contradicts the assumption that regulations kill jobs; with wetland and conservation banking, the regulations create jobs.

In response to recent directives, the Corps of Engineers and Environmental Protection Agency are planning to redefine what wetlands and waters are regulated by the Clean Water Act, which could reduce the extent of federal wetland regulation. USFWS has been directed to look at options to modify or eliminate the Endangered Species Act. It is important that more voices join the conversation and let elected officials know that environmental regulations were not put in place to get rid of jobs. Regulations were put in place by elected officials responding to public demands for clean water, clean air, soils that can grow plants, keeping water on the landscape to reduce flooding, eliminating the dead zone in the Gulf of Mexico, and many other reasons. We need to find solutions that allow for growth and prosperity without degrading or eliminating our resources completely. Wetlands should not be viewed as a nuisance to be conquered or eliminated, but on the other hand, we cannot expect to preserve every wetland and keep it from harm forever. Finding a reasonable pathway through the "swamp" will lead to greater conservation of our resources, especially when this pathway can bring together diverse interests for a common goal.

The importance of wetlands as habitat for all species, endangered and nonendangered, is well known throughout the biological and ecological communities, but it is less well known to many others. One reason for this is that biologists and ecologists live in a world of facts and figures exclusive to their fields and are not good at communicating the relevance of their work to everyday life. The task of compiling this scattered information, relating it to the world around us, and communicating an informed message to the public is often left to others. Artists, such as those highlighted in this book, help raise awareness about our endangered species by making them relatable and tangible. The endangered species intricately represented as fiber art in this book are no longer just names and descriptions in journal articles; they are brought to life and made real by the artists.

For me, playing in and exploring wetlands and natural areas was a huge part of my childhood and early learning experience. Like most kids, I was drawn to areas where water and land meet, where life is diverse and interesting, and where many endangered species are found for the same reasons. If we work to raise awareness, make our natural resources relevant to daily life, share our knowledge and interests, and find opportunities to work with others we might not always agree with, I believe we can dispel the notion that the swamp must be drained.

John Overland
Professional Wetland Scientist
Brainerd, Minnesota
May 24, 2018

OREGON SPOTTED FROG

Bobbie Dewees, Springfield, Virginia

- *Rana pretiosa*
- Chordata/Amphibia
- Vulnerable: population decreasing
- Medium-size frog ranges from 1.75 to 4 inches in length. The body color changes with age. Adults turn reddish brown with ragged black spots.
- They are located in or near bodies of water with vegetation, from southern British Columbia to southern Oregon.
- According to egg mass surveys at Conboy Lake National Wildlife Refuge, this frog is among the amphibian species most at risk in western North America. Habit loss is occurring due to development. Another reason for a decreasing population is the introduction of new species, such as bullfrogs, warm-water fishes, and reed canary grass. Changes in hydrology lead to variances in the timing and amount of rainfall and snowmelt, due to climate change, and there have been man-made modifications done for irrigation purposes. The irrigation systems associated with development are contrary to favorable frog habitat.
- At Conboy Lake, attempts are being made to remove introduced bullfrogs and fish, as well as preventing further introduction: fish and bullfrogs are predators and competitors for the Oregon spotted frog. Conservationists are working to manage canary grass. The frogs prefer to lay eggs in reed canary grass, but the grass has grown too thick. In the private sector, lawsuits are pending in the US District Court brought by environmental groups to force the federal government to ensure that these frogs have enough water to survive.

ORNATE EAGLE RAY

Elly Dyson, Annandale, Virginia

- *Aetomylaeus vespertilio*
- Chordata/Chondrichthyes
- Endangered: population decreasing
- Greenish brown colored with decorative dark stripes and white spots on body. Size reaches just under 8 feet, and its long tail can grow to body length. The tail does not contain barbs; this species is harmless to humans. Their diet is snails, mussels, and crustaceans. They are rarely observed, and their life span is 15 years.

- Lives in parts of the Indian Ocean, the western Pacific Ocean, and the South China Sea, usually in muddy banks, inshore coral reefs, and shallow waters
- Widely used for meat and cartilage, these rays are caught by fishermen and fisheries.
- To revive this species, laws need to be made and enforced, in order to manage the harvest and trade. At this time, no conservation measures exist.

OYSTER MUSSEL

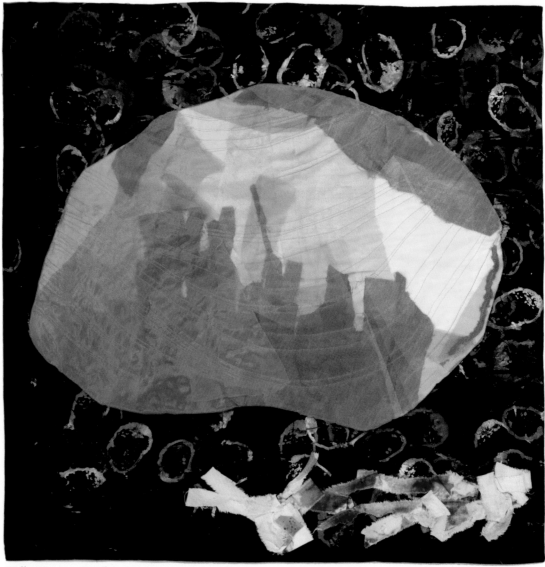

Willa Downes, Fairfax, Virginia

- *Epioblasma capsaeformis*
- Chordata/Mollusca
- Endangered: population decreasing
- This mollusk has a dull to shiny shell with dark-green rays. They are 2.75 inches long.
- They live in shallow water along the Tennessee and the Cumberland Rivers.

- They are becoming extinct because their habitats have been altered and polluted by humans. Rivers are dammed or channeled and sedimentation has occurred; harmful pollutants include ammonia and residue from coal mining.
- Remaining habitat needs to be improved. Information should be given to local populations so they can help keep waterways clean.

PACIFIC POCKET MOUSE

Lisa Arthaud, Warrenton, Virginia

- *Perognathus longimembris* subsp. *pacificus*
- Mammalia/Heteromyidae
- Critically Endangered, according to USFWS, they were believed to be extinct for nearly 20 years; upon rediscovery, they received full protection status in 1994.
- This is the smallest mouse species in North America; adults weigh a quarter of an ounce. They are nocturnal and live in sandy, coastal, sage scrub ecoregions, within 4 miles of the ocean.
- Endemic to California, they inhabit the coastal lands in Camp Pendleton and at Dana Point.

- Numbers are precarious due to habit destruction caused by urban, agricultural, residential, and recreational sprawl.
- In 2011, it was determined that these mice could not be recovered by remaining in the wild. Collaboration among federal, state, and regional partners resulted in the Pacific Pocket Mouse Recovery Program at the San Diego Zoo Institute for Conservation Research. This effort has resulted in successful captive breeding.

Susannah Kipp, Great Cacapon, West Virginia

Paiute Cutthroat Trout

- *Oncorhynchus clarkia* subsp. *seleniris*
- Chordata/Actinopterygii
- Not evaluated by the IUCN Red List but listed as Threatened by the USFWS; population trend is increasing.
- These trout are copper colored and have a few faded spots. They get up to 10 inches long and weigh up to a pound. They prefer a stream pool habitat with overhanging banks and abundant vegetation. Their diet consists of insects, and their life span is less than five years.
- They are endemic to a 9-mile stretch of Silver King Creek and tributaries in California's Sierra Nevada.
- They are considered threatened because of crossbreeding with nonnative trout. Populations are isolated from each other, limiting genetic diversity. There is habitat degradation due to sheep and cattle grazing.
- All grazing has been stopped in the Silver King Creek basin. In a controversial step, biologists poisoned a remote Sierra stream, attempting to get rid of all hybridized and nonnative trout. Afterward, the dead fish were removed, the stream was chemically neutralized, and more Paiute cutthroat trout were reintroduced.

PENDANT KIHI FERN

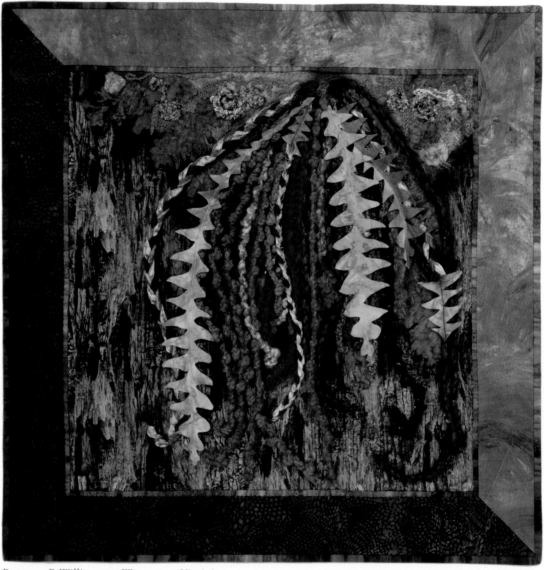

Rosanne F. Williamson, Warrenton, Virginia

- *Adenophorus periens*
- Plantae/Grammitis family
- Critically Endangered: population trend decreasing
- This plant, with long fronds that descend 15 inches or more, is epiphytic in nature, which means it grows on the surface of another plant. In this case, these ferns grow on trees. The yellow-green fronds have leaves lined with tiny hairs; the wind disperses the spores.
- Found in the lowland forest on the Big Island of Hawaii, they prefer shade and humidity.

- At risk because of lava and gas from volcanic activity and subsequent death of host trees, competition for remaining habitat by invasive nonnative species, and predation and habitat destruction by cattle and pigs.
- Conservationists continue to survey populations; their remaining habitat needs protection. A volcanic-hazard contingency plan should be developed so plants are rescued before being destroyed by volcanic events. Cultivation has not yet been successful.

Cheryl Stanczyk, Beavercreek, Ohio

- *Pithecophaga jefferyi* (also known as the monkey-eating eagle)
- Chordata/Aves
- Critically Endangered: population trend decreasing
- At more than 3 feet tall and weighing up to 9 pounds, this is the world's largest eagle. It has a grayish beak, is brown with a white belly, and has long feathers forming a distinctive shaggy crest. Their legs are strong and yellow, with powerful claws. They eat lemurs, monkeys, rodents, squirrels, birds, bats, and domestic animals. Their life span is between 30 to 60 years.
- Endemic to forests on a number of islands in the Philippines

- Deforestation is causing loss of habitat; they require the canopy of the forest to survive. Other factors affecting their demise include pollution, hunting, and collection.
- CITES restricts international trade. The Philippine Eagle Conservation Programme promotes education, protection, and monitoring. The punishment for the killing of an eagle is 12 years in prison. The Philippine Eagle Foundation of Davao City is an organization devoted to protection and conservation. These birds have been successfully bred in captivity.

Susan Price, Springfield, Virginia

- *Chlamyphorus truncatus*
- Chordata/Mammalia
- Listed as data deficient in IUCN Red List and designated Endangered by USFWS and Earth's Endangered Creatures; populations are decreasing.
- This creature is about 5 inches long and weighs a quarter of a pound. It has a rosy-colored shell on top of a white furry body. It spends its life burrowing through the earth, 6 inches below the surface, using its large claws to dig and its tail for balance. Their bodies are aerodynamically such that they seem to almost swim through the dirt. A superpower is that they are able to bury themselves in just seconds if threatened. They consume ant larvae, ants, worms, and plants. Living a solitary life, this armadillo rarely comes aboveground, except when it encounters ground too difficult to tunnel through. Most of these armadillos that are seen are trying to cross a road. They do not live for very long in captivity due to stress and an inability to adapt to an artificial diet.
- They are located in the deserts of Argentina.
- Threats include increasing development leading to loss of habitat. During the wet season, rain floods their tunnels and makes their fur wet, so they are unable to control body temperature. Another risk is aboveground predators, especially dogs.
- To revive the species, their habitat needs to be improved somehow. Unfortunately, they have not fared well in captivity.

Regina Grewe, Kamen, Germany

- *Porpolomopsis calyptriformis*
- Fungi/Basidiomycota
- Not evaluated by IUCN but appears on national red lists of Threatened fungi in Europe
- These mushrooms have a pinkish-lilac conical cap, 1 to just over 2 inches in diameter. The delicate stems are 2 to 3 inches in length.
- They grow in unimproved grasslands, lawns, and fields and at the edges of woods in Europe, Asia, and North America.
- In decline due to destruction, use of fertilizer, and pollution of grassland habitats.

- To avoid damaging their habitats, avoid the use of fertilizers and other chemicals. On enriched grassland sites, mowing and removing the cut grass over an extended period (at least 10 years, but probably nearer to 30 years) will gradually restore the habitat quality. Then it is hoped that waxcap mushrooms will recolonize these sites. The UK Biodiversity Action Plan is working to maintain and increase populations. They are included in the English Nature's Species Recovery Programme.

PIPING PLOVER

Laura Robertson, Kearneysville, West Virginia

- *Charadrius melodus*
- Chordata/Aves
- Near Threatened, with populations increasing, according to the IUCN Red List. Federally Endangered, according to the USFWS.
- This is a 7-inch-long, stocky shorebird that has orange legs and a sand-colored body. They eat bugs and crustaceans.
- Lives on sandy or rocky beaches in the US and parts of Canada and Mexico

- Species is at risk because of degradation of their beach habitat due to development and pollution by the oil and gas industries.
- Intensive management and protection of beach habitat have led to the increase in population. Protection needs to continue to maintain the growing trend of this species.

Ellen Fisher, Hollis, New Hampshire

- *Clarkis speciosa* subsp. *immaculate*
- Plantae/Onagraceae family
- Not evaluated by IUCN, federally listed as Endangered
- This flowering plant has purple-pink blossoms about an inch in diameter, and red wirelike stems. It is approximately 2 feet tall, both sprawling and sparse.
- Found in the chaparral near Pismo Beach in San Luis Obispo County, California. It grows on dry, sandy hills at low elevations.
- They are at risk because of habitat loss due to development.
- Steps toward possible revival could include monitoring existing populations and preventing further damage, educating the public, preserving new populations, and continuing to make the species available to gardeners.

Luana Rubin, Boulder, Colorado

POLAR BEAR

- *Ursus maritimus*
- Chordata/Mammalia
- Vulnerable: population trend decreasing
- This is a carnivorous bear. They have adapted to live in extremely cold temperatures; their whitish coat, which yellows as the bear ages, is well insulated. Because they spend so much time on ice, they are classified as marine mammals. Excellent swimmers, able to swim for days, they spend half their time in search of food. Their diet is primarily seals, as well as beluga whales and narwhals. Males weigh between 700 to 1500 pounds and are roughly 8 to 10 feet tall. They are often solitary and are not territorial, having keen senses of sight, hearing, and especially smell. Their life span is up to 25 years.
- They live within the Arctic Circle, on the frozen Arctic Ocean and on Arctic land in Canada, the US (in Alaska), Russia, Norway, and Greenland.
- Polar bears are threatened because of climate change. The ice is melting, which means the bears cannot feed as much as they have in the past. Less reported is the effect of toxic contaminants. Pesticides, PCBs, industrial byproducts, and oil exposure can result in poisoning and the genetic disruption of health and reproduction, and the lowered survival of cubs. These toxins accumulate in the fat cells of bears and are passed on in a concentrated form through the mother's milk to the cubs. Even a small amount of oil (ingested through grooming fur or eating contaminated prey) can cause liver and kidney damage. Polar bears are an iconic species whose survival is being severely disrupted by habitat reduction and contamination.
- We should take action to stop further Arctic pollution and climate change. We should monitor and manage the production and dumping of toxic compounds and prevent possible exposure to oil and other contaminants.

Colleen Tavenner, Paw Paw, West Virginia

POPOLO KU MAI

- *Solanum incompletum*
- Plantae/Colanaceae family
- Critically Endangered: population trend decreasing
- This is a woody shrub with reddish prickles on the leaves. The oval leaves are lobed, with one to four lobes on each side. Star-shaped white flowers grow in loose branching clusters.
- Their habitats include dry shrublands, forest ridges, and gulches and on older lava flows on Maui, Lana'i, and the Big Island of Hawaii.
- Habitat degradation, fire, stochastic (randomly sequenced) extinction, and decreased reproductive vigor because only a small number of the species remain are causing populations to decline.
- Statewide and island conservation projects include surveying the historical range, establishing of secure ex situ stocks, and augmenting the wild population.

Proboscis Monkey

Cheryl Rounds, Vienna, Virginia

- *Nasalis larvatus*
- Chordata/Mammalia
- Endangered: population decreasing
- These monkeys are between 21 to 30 inches tall, and they weigh up to 50 pounds. The unusual feature of this mammal is the pendant-shaped nose of the male; it can exceed 4 inches and is used to attract females. Noses of females are shorter and more upturned. They have a pale-orange/brown fur coat, and the limbs and tail are gray. The face is hairless, and they subsist mostly on plants. This species is one of the most aquatic of all primates and is an adept diver and swimmer, having webbed fingers and toes.
- Found only in Borneo. They spend most of their time in trees in forests and mangroves, near bodies of water.
- The species is declining mostly because of loss of habitat; forests are being burned and converted to crop plantations, including oil palm. Predators include crocodiles in the water, and jaguars on land. Humans hunt them because some consider their meat a delicacy.
- There are 16 parks and reserves where these monkeys are protected, and where the habitats are maintained. There are stiff penalties for poaching, but it is difficult to catch poachers.

Przewalski's Horse

Kim Gibson, Burke, Virginia

- *Equus ferus* subsp. *przewalski* (also known as Asian wild horse)
- Chordata/Mammalia
- Endangered: population increasing
- This is a wild horse with slight genetic differences from domesticated horses; they have 66 chromosomes while domestics have 64. More live in captivity than in the wild; they were extinct in the wild at one time but have been reintroduced. These horses, weighing up to 660 pounds and standing 48 to 56 inches tall, are stocky, with shorter legs than domestic horses. They are brown colored with a darker-brown mane. They keep within eyesight of their herd and have many ways of communicating with one another.

- Found in Mongolia, China
- They are at risk due to hunting, military activities in the area, climate change, and decline in the number of places where they can find water. They are in jeopardy because of hybridization with domestic species and loss of genetic diversity. Small population and restricted range are detrimental.
- This species is legally protected, and hunting is prohibited. A Species Survival Plan has been developed, and measures are being taken to minimize inbreeding and retain genetic diversity. Continued monitoring and training of biologists working with these horses are necessary.

Dana Brennan Hancock, Chantilly, Virginia

Puerto Rican Amazon

- *Amazona vittata*
- Chordata/Aves
- Critically Endangered: population increasing
- A medium-sized green parrot with red feathers near its beak; the eye has a large white eye ring, and the voice is very noisy. They make nests in hollow cavities of trees.
- Endemic to Puerto Rico, this is the only parrot found in the US. The wild population, which once lived throughout forests of the island, now lives only in El Yunque National Forest and Río Abajo State Forest.
- They are threatened with extinction because their forest habitat has been reduced for agriculture and road construction. Hurricanes are a serious danger, since they destroy the forest canopy where these parrots nest and feed. They are caught for the pet trade, killed for feed, and destroyed to reduce their impact on crop damage. There is competition for nest sites from other birds, illness from parasitic botflies, and danger from predators, including the pearly-eyed thrasher and red-tailed hawk.
- In 1968, the Puerto Rican Parrot Recovery Program was created. By 1973, captive breeding was underway at Luquillo Aviary. In 1975, only 13 of these parrots were found in the wild. There are now about 450 captive parrots. During Hurricanes Irma and Maria, they were kept safe in hurricane-proof rooms with suspended cages. Their caretakers lived with them for several days during and after Hurricane Maria. Because feeding areas were destroyed, they feed on the ground, but this makes them more vulnerable to predators. Workers at Luquillo and Río Abajo have constructed artificial feeding stations stocked with pellets and seeds. The forest is rejuvenating.

Eileen Doughty, Vienna, Virginia

PURPLE-FACED LANGUR

- *Trachypithecus vetulus*
- Chordata/Mammalia
- Endangered: population decreasing
- These monkeys have varied colored coats, grayish to brown/black, and the whiskers on their faces are lighter colored. Mostly arboreal, they weigh 10 to 20 pounds. They are 18 inches to 2 feet in length, with a 2-foot-long tail. They eat tree leaves and live in packs. Territorial, but living closely with other packs, the males of rival packs get into vicious battles. Their life span is around 23 years.
- Endemic to Sri Lanka; found in tropical rainforests and other areas with canopy cover, preferring to be close to water sources. When habitat is lost, groups seek shelter in residential gardens and on rubber plantations.
- Declining populations are blamed on habitat loss, which has caused artificially dense populations. Other threats include logging, human settlement, hunting, trade, agriculture, and deforestation.
- To revive the species, there needs to be habitat management, public education, government education, and implementation of current conservation laws. Population counts should be conducted because little is known about the species.

Elly Dyson, Annandale, Virginia

Pygmy Three-Toed Sloth

- *Bradypus pygmaeus*
- Chordata/Mammalia
- Critically Endangered: population decreasing
- This animal has a tan face with a dark band across the brow, rough hair on the crown and shoulders, and grayish limbs with three claws. It is 20 inches long, weighs less than 8 pounds, and lives most commonly in red mangrove trees, where it feeds on leaves.
- They are endemic on the Isla Escudo de Veraguas, a small island off the coast of Panama.
- Timber harvesting and human settlement are threatening their habitat, and there is a growing interest in collecting them for captivity as more people learn about them.
- Although the island is a protected wildlife refuge, that status should be better enforced, and an improved conservation plan should be put into place.

QUOKKA

Polly Maynard Davis, Warrenton, Virginia

- *Setonix brachyurus*
- Chordata/Mammalia
- Vulnerable: population trend decreasing
- Roughly the size of a domestic cat, the quokka is a small wallaby and a marsupial. They are nocturnal herbivores, 16 to 22 inches long and weigh 5.5 to 11 pounds. Their bodies are stocky and covered with brown fur. They can climb small trees and live for about 10 years. The baby lives in its mother's pouch for six months.
- The largest colony lives on Rottnest Island in Australia. They live near swamps with dense vegetation or scrubland.
- They are dying off because of animal predators (fox, feral cats, and feral pigs) and loss of habitat from logging and development. Disease is taking a toll. On the mainland, climate change is the biggest threat. The areas where they live are drying out, which reduces the swamplands on which quokkas depend.
- Two ways to increase awareness are to formally list the species as threatened under Australian law, and to establish protected areas. Researchers are studying population size, diet, and habitat use. Predator control needs to be established and maintained.

RAINBOW LEAF BEETLE

Linda T. Cooper, Burke, Virginia

- *Chrysolina cerealis*
- Arthropoda/Insecta
- Not evaluated by the IUCN Red List; Endangered and protected in the UK
- This is said to be the most beautiful beetle in all of the UK. It contains colorful red, green, and purple stripes. The males of this species are about a quarter of an inch, and the females are just a bit larger.
- They can be found in Eurasia.
- It is unknown for certain why they are so rare; studies are being done to investigate the role climate change might play.

- According to Dr. David Furth, a leaf beetle expert at the Smithsonian Museum of Natural History, often the declines in populations are due to decreases in food sources. Animal grazing is destroying wild thyme, an essential part of the leaf beetle habitat. Perhaps plants can be transplanted and animals can be led to graze on different plants.

RAINBOW PARROTFISH

Dabney Narvaez, Reston, Virginia

- *Scarus guacamaia*
- Chordata/Actinopterygii
- Near Threatened: population decreasing
- Parrotfish are a keystone species. This species is the largest herbivorous fish in the Atlantic; males grow to more than 4 feet in length. The teeth are fused to form a "beak." It uses its strong mouthparts to scrape algae and other plant matter from the surface of coral. This action benefits the fish as well as the coral. They have a life span of seven years, and during their lives they can change color, shape, and gender.

- They are found in the western Atlantic Ocean, from Florida to Argentina, and are dependent on mangroves.
- One reason for population decline is that mangroves are being lost. Pollution is poisoning them, there is coral reef loss and coastal development, and overfishing (often spearfishing) is detrimental.
- In Bermuda, they are protected. Protective measures should be expanded. Marine reserves are being established, and further monitoring is recommended. Limit mangrove removal.

RED PANDA

Linda P. Keithley, Centreville, Virginia

- *Ailurus fulgens* (also known as the lesser panda)
- Chordata/Mammalia
- Endangered: population decreasing
- This animal is bearlike, with russet fur on the upper body. The belly and limbs are black, and there are white markings above the eyes. It has a long, bushy tail with darker shades of russet rings. They have big, round heads; large, pointy ears; and a short snout. They weigh 6.5 to 14 pounds, are around 25 inches long, and have a 15-inch tail. They are excellent tree climbers and have uniquely flexible ankles. In fact, their fibulas completely rotate on their axes. They were initially thought to belong to the raccoon family but then were reassigned to the bear family. Further study classifies them as neither bear nor raccoon, but they closely resemble weasels, skunks, and raccoons. They feed mostly on bamboo.
- Native to the eastern Himalayas and southwestern China
- They are often caught in traps intended for deer, and then killed. They are victims of poaching for their pelts, which are used for hats. Loss of nesting trees and bamboo has resulted from forest clearing.
- To revive the species, laws must be passed to prohibit the sale of products containing their pelts. The forests need to be protected.

Pat Washburn, Chantilly, Virginia

RED-COCKADED
WOODPECKER

- *Leuconotopicus borealis*
- Chordata/Aves
- Near Threatened; federally classified as Endangered by USFWS; population trend seems to be increasing.
- This is a 7-to-9-inch black-and-white bird, with a wingspan of about 15 inches. Adult males have a red strip on both sides of their heads, and white cheeks. They have been known to live up to 12 years, but their average life span is shorter. This bird eats bugs and spiders from the bark of trees. It makes its nest high up in mature longleaf pine trees, boring a hole high in a living tree, usually infected with red heart fungus. The disease allows for easier evacuation of the hole. After making a nest as large as needed, the woodpecker makes holes around the opening to allow the flow of sap. This acts to deter predators. A typical clutch is from two to four eggs. Living in a cooperative family community, parents and other mature birds share incubation and feeding responsibilities. Newborn woodpeckers require a fresh insect about every five minutes all day long.
- They are at risk because of loss of habitat due to logging, agriculture, and development.
- Steps to save this species include limiting access to breeding areas, restricting logging and building, controlling the understory in pine forests, managing forest density, replanting trees, banding and monitoring fledglings, relocating juvenile birds to start new communities, and making artificial nests for breeding.

RED-CROWNED CRANE

Ann Clare, Alexander, North Carolina

- *Grus japonensis*
- Chordata/Aves
- Endangered: population trend decreasing
- These birds are approximately 5 feet tall and weigh 17 to 22 pounds; this is the heaviest species of cranes. They have white primary feathers, black secondary feathers, and bare red skin on the forehead and crown. This is an aquatic bird that forages in coastal marshes, rivers, rice paddies, and other cultivated fields. Nests are built on wet ground or in shallow water.
- Found in East Asia, primarily Japan, Korea, and China. Their breeding habitat is farther inland along the Russia-China border.
- Facing extinction because agricultural expansion, deforestation, and land development are destroying their habitat. Use of pesticides is poisoning them.
- Steps need to be taken to continue to protect the wetlands.

REINDEER

Tamara Webb, Ashburn, Virginia

- *Rangifer tarandus*
- Chordata/Mammalia
- Vulnerable: population trend decreasing
- This species of deer can reach almost 50 inches in height and 90 inches in length and weighs 120 to 700 pounds. They have short tails, and both males and females have antlers. Their coloration varies between seasons but is usually medium to light brown. They have wide hooves, which are helpful in the snow and tundra for digging, and when swimming. They eat plants, grasses, roots, bark, and lichen. Their superpower is that they are said to travel distances of over 3,000 miles a year, which is more than any other terrestrial mammal. They travel in herds for safety from predators—bear and wolves. They can run up to 50 miles per hour, and their life span is 5 to 15 years.

- Located around the Arctic regions in the northwestern US, Canada, Greenland, Norway, Finland, Russia, and Mongolia. Migratory in nature, they inhabit mountain ranges, coastal plains, tundra, and boreal forests.
- Population decline due to climate change and subsequent landscape changes, particularly in the Arctic. They are at risk because of development in their habitat, involving energy plants, tourist resorts, road building, mining, forestry, and industrialization. Other risks include animal predation and hunting by humans.
- Herds need to be tracked and monitored, and special management planning should focus on habitat degradation, protected areas, predation management, and hunting regulation. Setting aside land for national parks can be part of the problem rather than a solution, because subsequently increased tourism and recreational activity greatly disrupt animals in the natural world.

Lois Sovey, Herndon, Virginia

- *Lemur catta*
- Chordata/Mammalia
- Endangered: population trend decreasing
- This is a diurnal primate species, weighing between 5 and 8 pounds. Their bodies are almost 18 inches long, and their distinctive black-and-white-striped tail is more than 21 inches long. They have slim fingers with humanlike nails. Herbivores, they explore trees and the ground and are social creatures, living in groups of six to 30 lemurs, called troops. A dominant female presides over the troop. They have many different vocalizations, including purring and alarm calls. A superpower: males have a scent-marking ability, and they get into "stink fights" by waving their tail at rivals. Malagasy legends tell stories of lemurs as souls of their ancestors.
- They are located on the African island of Madagascar, and on other surrounding islands.
- These animals are becoming extinct due to farming, livestock, and charcoal production. The forests they inhabit are disappearing. They are at risk because they are hunted and poached for the exotic pet trade.
- This is the most common primate held in captivity in zoos, labs, and the pet trade. They breed well in captivity, and reintroduction into the wild is possible. There are several existing protected areas in the wild, and visiting students and locals are helping with field research and resource management. Ecotourism is beneficial.

Rock Gnome Lichen

Kathryn Gray, Manassas, Virginia; Nancy Karst, Springfield, Virginia

- *Cetradoni linearis*
- Fungi/Lecanoromycetes family
- Vulnerable: population decreasing
- This lichen has narrow strap-like lobes on vertical rock faces, where water seeps from above.
- Found in North Carolina and Asia
- In jeopardy because of soil erosion and soil damage by hikers and nature lovers
- Educate hikers to stay on trails.

RUGEL'S PAWPAW

Lynn Chinnis, Oro Valley, Arizona

- *Deeringothamnus rugelii*
- Plantae/Annonaceae family
- Critically Imperiled, according to NatureServe
- This is a low shrub with faintly scented cream to purplish six-petaled flowers.
- Endemic to Volusia County, Florida, in poorly drained pine-saw palmetto grassy flatlands

- Development and conversion of land to turf farms and pine plantations have led to endangerment. Root destruction is fatal to this species.
- Most remaining plants are in parks and conservation lands, where they can be managed by mowing, controlled burns, or both.

Kris A. Bishop, Woodbridge, Virginia

- *Bombus affinis*
- Arthropoda/Insecta
- Critically Endangered: population trend decreasing
- These large bees have a rusty-colored patch on the middle section of the abdomen.
- Located in North America, mostly in the Midwest to eastern US. Found in grasslands, marshes, agricultural areas, and residential parks and gardens. Their nests are often underground in abandoned rodent nests or aboveground in the grass, old bird nests, or piles of rocks or in holes of dead trees.
- Pollution, herbicide and pesticide use, parasites, and climate change are causes of habitat loss and subsequent decline of these bees. Plagued by stressors such as reduced food and hibernation sites. An abundance of rodents may limit nesting sites. Bees emerge from hibernation early, causing stress. They have distinct nutritional needs; one of these is a large, constant supply of flowers blooming from April through September. The amount of pollen available during this season directly affects the number of queens produced.
- This species could be helped by freeing grasslands and bee sites of pesticides, grazing, and other habitat threats.

RUTHVENS KINGSNAKE

Marcie Sterrett Schoonmaker, Centreville, Virginia

- *Lampropeltis rutheni*
- Chordata/Reptilia
- Near Threatened: population trend decreasing
- This is a harmless little snake, up to 30 inches long, with brilliant red, black, and either white/yellow or gray stripes. Its "look-alike" poisonous snake is the coral snake, discernible by the order of the colored stripes.
- They are located in tropical and subtropical forests and farmlands in Mexico.

- Deforestation due to agricultural farming, construction of roads and railroads, and commercial hunting and trapping for the sometimes-illegal pet trade are causing a decline in the population.
- Habitat needs to be researched, monitored, and planned. Water protection, species management techniques, and establishing protection agreements with private landowners are necessary.

SAN JOAQUIN KIT FOX

Crystal Rousseau, Stafford, Virginia

- *Vulpes macrotis* subsp. *mutica*
- Chordata/Mammalia
- Listed on the IUCN Red List as least concern; ESA says it is Endangered.
- This is the smallest fox in North America; body length is approximately 20 inches and it weighs 5 pounds. It has long legs, a bushy tail, and large ears and is mostly nocturnal.

- Located in California
- The habitat is being diminished because what were once grasslands are now farms and urban areas.
- Defenders of Wildlife is working together with the California Rangeland Conservation Coalition to save the grasslands.

SANDPLAIN GERARDIA

Dottie Dane, Annandale, Virginia

- *Agalinis acuta*
- Plantae/Orobanchaceae family
- Listed as Critically Impaired by NatureServe
- This plant grows to only 4 to 8 inches, containing flowers no larger than a dime. The thin, nonserrated leaves occur opposite each other on the stem. It somewhat resembles the rosemary plant.
- They are located on Atlantic coastal sand plains from Cape Cod to Maryland, though they are not found in Connecticut, New Jersey, or Delaware. Their habitat is marine grassland: open spaces without larger plants encroaching.
- Humans are building residential, commercial, and recreational developments in what were open areas along the sands. Historically, cattle grazing and natural fires kept down the other vegetation that usually crowds out gerardia. They are exploited for commercial or educational use.
- Regulation is necessary to protect this species. In the 1980s, the natural-resources agencies in New York, New England, and the USFWS conducted field surveys in conjunction with the Nature Conservancy and botanical associations, and they devised a recovery plan. They worked with the New England Wildflower Society to cultivate a population for collection of seeds. Seeds are planted on backsides of dunes, where there is no damaging pedestrian traffic.

SCALLOPED HAMMERHEAD SHARK

Kathy Edwards, Alexandria, Virginia

- *Sphyrna lewini*
- Chordata/Chondrichthyes
- Endangered
- This shark is distinguished from other hammerheads by a central indentation on the anterior margin of the head, along with two more indentations on each side of this central indentation. This characteristic is what gives the head a "scalloped" appearance. These sharks are seldom found in waters colder than 71°F. They have been documented as entering enclosed bays and estuaries. Diet consists of bony fish, octopus, squid, and baitfish.
- They can be found in many parts of the world but have all but disappeared in temperate and tropical seas. In the western Atlantic Ocean, the range extends from the northeast coast of the US to Brazil. In the eastern Atlantic, they can be found from the Mediterranean to Namibia. Populations exist in the Indian Ocean and in the western Pacific. Distribution in the Pacific Ocean extends from the coast of Southern California to Ecuador, and off the waters of Hawaii and Tahiti.
- Populations are at risk due to overfishing and demand for shark fins. Fins are used to make a delicacy, shark fin soup. Juveniles are targeted for their meat. The mostly unregulated catch off West Africa, threats from overexploitation and poor management, and the rising demand for food and protein in this region (projected to double by 2020) contribute significantly to the risk of extinction.
- These sharks are used to prepare food delicacies, so it would take discipline for humans to avoid consumption to ensure greater livelihood. Unless the people of West Africa can find another protein food source, fish will continue to be their diet mainstay.

Jane Frenke, Berkeley Springs, West Virginia

SHENANDOAH SALAMANDER

- *Plethodon shenandoah*
- Chordata/Amphibia
- Vulnerable: population stable
- Only 4 inches in length, this nocturnal salamander absorbs oxygen through the water because it has no lungs. They may survive for 25 years and play an important role in ecology regarding insect predation and soil aeration. They are a food source for other animals.
- Endemic to Shenandoah National Park, in particular forested areas at high, cooler elevations
- Forests are subject to invasion of nonnative insects and disease. This leads to major impacts on tree mortality, which alters the entire habitat. The forest is experiencing climate change. Visitors to the park, in particular hikers and campers, are disruptive and this has a detrimental effect.
- In order to help the species survive, scientists are working to learn more about them. Part of this work includes monitoring. Park personnel are trying to figure out ways for park visitors to have less impact.

SHORT-TAILED CHINCHILLA

Darlene A. Narango, Berkeley Springs, West Virginia

- *Chinchilla chinchilla*
- Chordata/Mammalia
- Endangered: population trend decreasing
- This creature is a medium-sized rodent, 11 to 19 inches long and weighing just under 2 pounds, with a squirrel-like body, bushy tail, and large eyes. They have short front legs and strong back legs, perfect for jumping and climbing. They dig under rocks and in the ground, eat plants, have thick fur, and are social animals.

- They live in the Andes of South America, particularly in Bolivia and Chile.
- Hunting and poaching are causing their decline. Their pelts are highly sought, and their habitat is threatened.
- Their habitat should be restored, and we must expand the areas of protection. An agreement was signed by Andean countries to prohibit their capture, trade, and export. They should not be removed from the wild.

SILVERSTONE'S POISON FROG

Pat Washburn, Chantilly, Virginia

- *Ameerega silverstonei*
- Chordata/Amphibia
- Endangered: population trend decreasing
- These small frogs average from 1 to 2 inches long, and they exhibit some of the most vibrant colors in the animal kingdom. They are red, orange, or yellow and have black spots. Their vivid colors serve as camouflage. They often lose this coloration in captivity. Their head is as wide as their body, and the nose is rounded and sloped. They are active during the day, foraging in debris next to streams or under leaves for small insects, mites, and termites. Lacking webbed feet, they are not good swimmers. They lay small clutches of five to six eggs. When threatened, a toxin is secreted as a deterrent.
- Endemic to Peru in the Cardillera Azul, Huanuco tropical rainforest region, at elevations of 1,200 feet and higher. They are not found in water but prefer damp, cool floors of undisturbed forests.
- Tadpoles often fall prey to other amphibians, reptiles, or predatory invertebrates, since they are not able to produce toxins until they are mature. Loss of habitat for urbanization has an adverse effect on populations. Agricultural activities and illegal pet trade are threats.
- Conservation efforts must include preserving their habitat, enforcing smuggling laws, and conducting more research.

SILVERSWORD

Kathleen Schneider-Braus, Middleton, Wisconsin

- *Argyroxyphium sandwisense*
- Plantae/Asteraceae family
- Vulnerable: population trend increasing
- This plant has many swordlike succulent leaves covered with silver hairs that make it highly adapted to extreme wind and high-altitude temperatures they endure. They have a long life span, sometimes more than 50 years, during which time they flower, producing tall stalks of maroon flowers resembling the sunflower. Then the plant goes to seed and dies.
- They grow only on the island of Maui in the Haleakala National Park, at elevations of 7,000 to 10,000 feet.
- Excessive grazing by nonnative animals has put this plant at risk. Vandalism by humans has resulted in near extinction.
- The National Park Service has educated one to two million annual visitors to the park, warning that harvesting or disturbance of these rare protected plants is illegal. The Haleakala Resource Management Division constructed and maintains 65 miles of fence to prevent the destruction of the plant by predatory mammals. This strict monitoring and government protection are considered a successful conservation story; however, new threats have emerged. Climate change will place the mountaintop species at severe risk of extinction. Warmer and drier conditions on the mountain signify a bleak outlook for the silversword. Future rainfall patterns on the mountain are difficult to predict. The Pacific Island Climate Change Cooperative is investigating genetic differences in subpopulations regarding drought tolerance. They are collaborating with Haleakala National Park to do outplanting into more-extensive environments, including wetter areas of the park, in hopes that the plant may survive.

SINGAPORE FRESHWATER CRAB

Dena Gail Brannen, Reston, Virginia

- *Johora singaporensis*
- Arthropoda/Malacostraca
- Critically Endangered
- This crab grows up to 12 inches and is a trapezoidal shape. It is primarily an aquatic species, easily distinguished from other freshwater crabs in Singapore by light and dark banding patterns on its walking legs and by the fields of short hairlike setae covering its body and legs.
- Located in Singapore and found only in a few freshwater hill streams in isolated forest areas in the vicinity of Bukit Timah, Bukit Batok, and Bukit Gombak
- They are in danger because of the degradation of their habitat, including the reduction in water quality, the drying up of streams, and the damage by various human activities.
- Their remaining habitat needs to be protected, and there should be establishment of captive breeding populations to revive this species.

SLENDER CHUB

Katherine Heslep, Alexandria, Virginia

- *Erimystax cahni*
- Chordata/Actinopterygii
- Endangered: population declining
- This fish is about 3.5 inches long. It is food for larger fish and is used for bait.
- They are located near the Tennessee-Virginia border in shallow, gravelly rivers with clean water.

- In decline due to loss of habitat, which is threatened by siltation, dredging, pollution, and water withdrawal. Coal silt from coal-washing operations is harmful.
- Reduce coal silt runoff and decrease water removal. More research is needed to learn more about reproduction habits and to reduce sediment inputs. Disturbance of the natural substrate should be prevented.

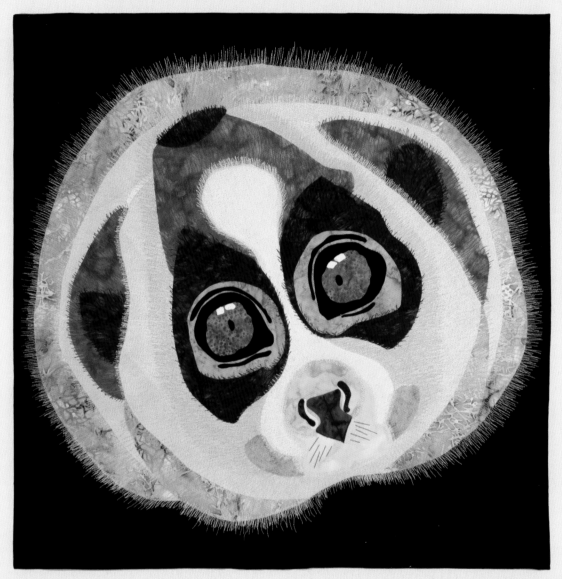

Meggan Czapiga, Schwenksville, Pennsylvania

- *Nycticebus coucang*
- Chordata/Mammalia
- Vulnerable: population trend decreasing
- These are small- to medium-sized nocturnal omnivore primates. The name "loris" is Dutch and means "clown"; this probably refers to their facial features. They have a round head, very large eyes, and a variety of distinctive coloration patterns. The loris is unusual because it is a venomous mammal, whose bite is toxic and dangerous to humans.
- Home is in South and Southeast Asia, across India and the Philippines, and into parts of Indonesia.
- They are disappearing due to habitat loss, but mostly because of hunting for the illegal pet trade and traditional medicine trade.
- Conservation groups are working hard, trying to stop trade. Surveys need to determine existing population densities and habitat viability. Tourists can help stamp out the pet trade by not paying for a photo with a loris and by not buying one as a pet. Social media is playing a huge role in fueling this cruel trade. Because the animal is so cute, videos of pet lorises are some of the most frequently watched animal-related viral videos. Do not view or share videos of seemingly cute pet show lorises; this is exploitation.

Marcie Sterrett Schoonmaker, Centreville, Virginia

Small Whorled Pogonia

- *Isotria medeoloides*
- Plantae/Orchidacea family
- Vulnerable: population trend decreasing
- This small plant grows to about 10 inches tall and has a whorl of five or six leaves beneath single or paired yellow-green flowers that are 1 to 3.5 inches. Grows under older hardwood trees and hemlock and prefers acidic soil created by thick layers of leaves.
- Located in 18 eastern US states and in Ontario, Canada
- In peril because of destruction to their habit through urban expansion, construction of roads, recreational activities, inadvertent damage by hikers, and commercial or personal collection
- Monitor and investigate habitat management techniques. Establish protection agreements with private landowners.

Bonnie Anderson, Haymarket, Virginia

SMOOTH CONEFLOWER

- *Echinacea laevigata*
- Plantae/Asteraceae family
- Designated Endangered by USFWS
- Perennial herb, flowering from May to July. Develops seeds from late June through September. It grows up to 3.3 feet tall, with a solitary flower head consisting of 13 to 21 light-pink to purple drooping petals up to 6 inches long, which grow from a conical seed head. Requires partial to full sun in well-drained open areas of neutral to alkaline soil; does not tolerate the close growth of taller plants.
- Located in 10 counties in Virginia, North Carolina, and Georgia
- Habitat destruction results from highway construction, residential and commercial development, roadside maintenance and cutting for utility rights-of-way, frequent mowing, and herbicides.
- Revival might be possible with purposeful planting in open areas, away from woody plants. Infrequent mowing, prescribed burning, and access by large herbivores are beneficial measures. Planting close to other species of echinacea should be avoided.

Ricki Selva, Fort Myer, Virginia

Snow Leopard

- *Panthera uncia*
- Chordata/Mammalia
- Vulnerable: population trend decreasing
- An elusive predator, generally solitary except for mothers raising cubs. They weigh around 95 pounds and have several adaptations for cold climates: plush coat, stocky body, long tail with thick fur, large paws, and elongated nostrils. Their coats are perfectly camouflaged for snowy and rocky habitats. They eat ibex, argali, and Himalayan blue sheep.
- Located at "the Roof of the World": the highest mountain ranges of central Asia, including Afghanistan, Bhutan, China, India, Kazakhstan, Kyrgyzstan, Mongolia, Nepal, Pakistan, Russia, Tajikistan, and Uzbekistan
- They are at risk due to poaching, loss of prey species, conflict with farmers, illegal trade, habitat fragmentation and destruction as a result of climate change, encroachment of development, border fences, mining, and logging.
- To revive the species, prevent poaching, including improving enforcement and transboundary protection. Reduce human-wildlife conflict, educate the indigenous communities so they will learn about grazing management, animal husbandry, and improving corrals. Consider incentive and compensatory payment to farmers; obtain livestock insurance. Encourage ecotourism to supplement income of residents in snow leopard habitat. Manage trophy-hunting practices.

Gay Bitter, Princeton, New Jersey

SOUTH ISLAND WREN

- *Xenicus gilviventris*
- Chordata/Aves
- Endangered: population trend decreasing
- This little ground-feeding bird has a short tail and rounded wings and is dull green to olive brown.
- They reside in the rocky alpine and subalpine areas of New Zealand's South Island.
- Threatened due to human settlement and the introduction of nonnative predators; increase in predation by stoats and mice may be due to climate change. Severe weather has a detrimental impact.
- Translocation to Anchor and Secretary Islands, where no invasive predatory species are present, is a good possibility for conservation.

Karen Coan, Birmingham, Michigan

SOUTHERN ROCKHOPPER PENGUIN

- *Eudyptes chrysocome*
- Chordata/Aves
- Vulnerable: population trend decreasing
- This is one of the smallest penguins; they weigh 4.5 to 6.5 pounds and are around 20 inches tall. They have a crest of yellow and black feathers, blood-red eyes, and pink feet.
- They live on rocky coastlines in the Falkland Islands, Argentina, Chile, and New Zealand.
- Commercial overfishing has reduced prey availability. Climate changes resulting in rising sea-surface temperatures and pollution have made for harsh conditions for these birds.
- Much research and monitoring are underway to assess trends in the population decline. Genetic studies are being conducted. International agreements are being implemented to hone marine protected areas and to regulate practices regarding fisheries, oil drilling, and other marine activities. Increased awareness is essential to educate children and their teachers about the effects of climate change and to suggest ways the public can help.

Ricki Selva, Fort Myer, Virginia

SOUTHERN SEA OTTER

- *Enhydra lutris* subsp. *nereis*
- Chordata/Mammalia
- Species is Endangered, according to IUCN; subspecies is Threatened, according to USFWS; population trend decreasing.
- Largest member of the weasel family and the second-smallest marine mammal, sea otters have webbed feet, and nostrils and ears that close in the water. Their thick, water-repellent fur traps air to form an insulating layer against chilly waters. Adults weigh between 50 to 100 pounds and must eat at least 25 percent of their body weight in prey each day. In the wild, their life span is 10 to 20 years. A sea otter may spend its entire life in the water or only occasionally comes onshore. This otter is a keystone species; they eat sea urchins, which cause seagrass beds and kelp forests to thrive and absorb large quantities of carbon dioxide from the atmosphere. They are an important sentinel species, which is an indicator of a danger to human life by providing early warnings. When these species are abundant in an area, this indicates certain environmental conditions, or suitable conditions that exist for a group of other species.
- Located along the coasts of the Pacific Ocean in North America and Asia
- These otters were believed to be completely extinct until a small group was discovered in the Big Sur area on the California coast. This subspecies has very little genetic diversity. They are vulnerable to oil spills, infectious diseases, parasites, boat strikes, entanglements, toxins, and shark attacks.
- Continued protection, advocacy, rescue, monitoring, and research are necessary. Improve water quality and overall health of California's coastal watersheds; this will give the otters a chance to extend their range. Coastal communities can be of assistance by encouraging local water boards to seek higher standards for watershed health and to reduce harmful runoff into marine environments.

Priscilla Stultz, Williamsburg, Virginia

- *Gazella spekei*
- Chordata/Mammalia
- Endangered: population trend decreasing
- This is the smallest species of gazelle, standing 2 feet tall at the shoulders and weighing 24 to 40 pounds. Their coloration is delicate looking: light brownish, with black-and-white facial markings. They have a superpower that is not so delicate. When they sense danger, they can inflate the saggy skin on the top area of their nose to make a very loud honking sound. These are social animals, and they travel in two kinds of herds. One is a male in the company of a bevy of mating females. The other is a bachelor herd comprising young males who have not amassed their own harem yet. They live up to 12 years in the wild.

- Located at the Horn of Africa, in northern Somalia, and in grasslands and coastal and inland sand dunes
- The main reason for population decline is the loss of grazing land, due to competition with livestock. Drought is lessening their food source. Their many predators include cheetahs, hyenas, lions, wild dogs, leopards, and pythons. Hunting is uncontrolled. There is extreme political instability in their land, and some regard these as the "devil's livestock." Many are caught in illegal wildlife trade, and they are displayed stuffed in hotel lobbies. There is lack of protection in areas of civil unrest.
- No functioning protected areas exist within their range. There are small herds in captivity.

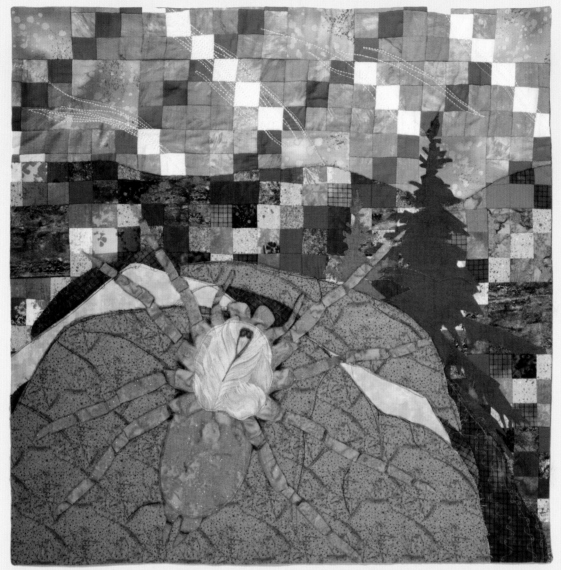

Susan Egge Haftel, Gainesville, Virginia

- *Microhexura montivaga*
- Arthropoda/Arachnid
- Not evaluated by IUCN but listed as Endangered by the Endangered Species Act; population trend in decline
- This is a tiny tarantula, around a tenth of an inch long. It eats flea-like organisms called springtails. These spiders construct funnel-shaped webs between moss and rock, but they don't appear to use the webs as traps for prey. It is theorized that their webs are more for shelter.
- Lives at high elevations in the Appalachian Mountains of North Carolina and Tennessee

- Trees that provide habitat for the spider's moss are infested by balsam woolly adelgids, tiny nonnative insects that kill fir trees. Forests where the spiders live have declined due to logging, storm damage, and wildfires. These spiders need moss mats to survive. The mats are fragile, requiring high and constant humidity; wind and rain ruin them. Regions where the spiders live are visited by thousands of hikers; inadvertent trampling takes a huge toll.
- Efforts are being made to protect and manage what populations remain. A captive breeding program might reestablish the spider. Scientists need to study this species more to better understand possible steps toward recovery.

STAGHORN CORAL

Kathryn Gray, Manassas, Virginia

- *Acropora cervicornis*
- Chordata/Anthozoa
- Critically Endangered: population stable
- This is a coral with cylindrical branches.
- Its habitat is coral reefs around the world.

- Disease, climate change, human-related factors, and thermal-induced bleaching all are adversely affecting the viability.
- Loss could be curtailed with greater protected areas and artificial propagation.

SUMATRAN ORANGUTAN

Kerry Faraone, Purcellville, Virginia

- *Pongo abelii*
- Chordata/Mammalia
- Critically Endangered: population decreasing
- These critters have a life span of over 50 years. Males are approximately 4.6 feet tall and are mostly solitary. Females are closer to 3 feet tall, and they are frequently in the company of their offspring. These orangutans spend most of their lives in trees, and they are diurnal. They eat fruit, especially figs, and parts of other plants, insects, and slow lorises. They play a critical role in dispersing seeds. It is feared that if the orangutans disappear, so will many tree species.
- They live in lowland and mountainous forests and peat swamps in Sumatra, Indonesia.
- Numbers are in decline because of deforestation for palm oil farming, logging, and building roads. They are poached and killed for encroaching on farms, and orphaned infants are sold in the illegal pet trade.
- Strict national laws in Indonesia make it illegal to capture, injure, kill, transport, or trade orangutans. Enforce these laws and protect forest areas from development.

Debbie Dempsey, Oak Hill, Virginia; Brenda Page, Herndon, Virginia

SUNDA PANGOLIN

- *Manis javanica*
- Chordata/Mammalia
- Critically Endangered: population trend decreasing
- Covered with scales, these mammals grow up to 4 feet and weigh up to 21 pounds. They are adept climbers, with prehensile tails and thick, powerful claws. Sundas ascend trees to reach arboreal ant nests or termite mounds. Having no teeth, pangolins use their long, sticky tongues, which are longer than their bodies, to collect insects. A pangolin consumes over 70 million insects per year. They have poor eyesight but rely on a great sense of smell to locate prey. They sleep in hollows of trees but are known to dig burrows in soil, where they give birth to one or two young each year. A superpower is that when they are threatened, pangolins roll into a ball to protect their soft underbellies. This species is rarely observed, mostly because of its increasing rarity, but also because it is secretive, elusive, and primarily nocturnal. They live to be about seven years old.
- This species is from southern China, Thailand, Vietnam, Cambodia, Sumatra, Java, and adjacent islands. They live in forests and can be found near oil palm and rubber plantations.
- Pangolins carry the tragic status of being the most trafficked mammal in the world. It has been estimated that over 1.1 million pangolins have been poached for the illegal trade in the last 16 years for use in traditional medicine and bush meat, and for demand in Asian markets, where they are eaten as a delicacy and used in traditional medicine. Their scales are used in an attempt to cure skin ailments, improve blood circulation, and stimulate milk secretion in lactating women, as well as in treating other ailments, including cancer. Their habitat is reduced due to increases in agriculture. Pangolins are preyed on by tigers and leopards. Their skins are used for boots, shoes, and other leather items.
- They are protected by most governmental jurisdictions. More effective enforcement of existing laws is critical for their conservation. Identification and verification of conservation efforts are crucial. More research into pangolin consumption is needed for preservation programs, especially in China. CITES recently increased protection of all pangolin species to the highest level, with the resolution taking effect in January 2017.

SWAMP PINK

Bunnie Jordan, Vienna, Virginia

- *Helonias bullata*
- Plantae/Liliaceae family
- Not evaluated by IUCN; designated Vulnerable by NatureServe
- This flowering plant is a perennial member of the lily family. A cluster of dark, oblong leaves can produce a 3-foot stalk topped by a cluster of small, pink flowers with pale-blue centers.
- Grows in forested wetlands from New Jersey to Georgia

- Populations are at risk due to wetland destruction and adjacent development, pollutant runoff, flooding, dam building by beavers, and climate change.
- Need preservation of wetlands, improved water quality and quantity, and management of sedimentation-generating activities. Redirecting vehicular and foot traffic would be helpful.

TANSY BEETLE

Lisa Dodson, Martinsville, Indiana

- *Chrysolina graminis*
- Chordata/Insecta
- Not evaluated by IUCN Red List; classified Endangered by the UK government and the Encyclopedia of Life
- Bright-green, coppery-colored insect that lives its entire life on or around the tansy plant
- Located along the banks of an 18-mile stretch of the River Ouse, York, in the United Kingdom. A much smaller population was recently found in Cambridgeshire. They live beside riverbanks or wetlands.
- Nonnative Himalayan balsam has rapidly expanded along riverbanks in areas where tansy beetles live. The result is that resident vital tansy plants have been crowded out.
- The Tansy Beetle Action Group initiates and oversees efforts toward conservation. Their efforts include removing Himalayan balsam, planting tansy plants, and thus creating safe havens. They work with landowners to reduce grazing of livestock, and they bring public awareness to the plight of this beetle.

Tina Lewis, Parker, Colorado

TAYLOR'S CHECKERSPOT BUTTERFLY

- *Euphydryas editha taylori*
- Arthropoda/Insecta
- Not evaluated by the IUCN Red List but listed as Endangered by the ESA
- This is an inland prairie species of butterfly, with a wingspan of 2.25 inches and short, stubby wings of black, orange, and white.
- Located in the northwestern US and Vancouver, British Columbia.
- Their habitat is lessening due to urban and agricultural development. Invasive species of trees and plants are spreading and taking over their habitat, and pesticide use and recreational activities are causing numbers to fall.
- To save the species, checkerspot conservation should include land management and conservation agencies, restoring the habitat, captive breeding, and reintroduction of species into favorable locales.

Jeanie Sakrison Velarde, Cordova, Tennessee

- *Panthera tigris*
- Chordata/Mammalia
- Endangered: population trend decreasing
- The largest of the cat species, these tigers are up to 11 feet long and can weigh as much as 670 pounds. They have a distinctive orange-colored coat, with vertical black stripes. They are territorial and solitary creatures with great strength. They have short, thick necks; wide shoulders; and huge paws with retractable claws. Their life span is 20 to 26 years.
- Most are in Asia: China, Nepal, Japan, South Korea, Thailand, Cambodia, Indonesia, India, and Bangladesh. Coincidentally, these happen to be some of the most populated areas in the world.
- They are at risk of extinction because of shrinking habitats. Agriculture, timber cutting, new road development, human settlement, industrial expansion, and hydroelectric dams are pushing the tigers into smaller and smaller areas. When their usual food sources disappear, they hunt livestock, and then humans kill them. Chinese medicine is becoming more popular because the standard of living in Southeast Asia has made it more available. Use of endangered tiger products and their medicines is seen as high status.
- Often, refuge areas are not large enough to support a tiger population. The refuges are hard to maintain, due to lack of funds and workforce. Since there are lucrative possibilities and high demand in tiger medicine and tiger pelts, the risk of poaching is perhaps worthwhile. Strict measures must be taken to thwart poachers; there is little optimism that this species can be saved.

Pamela Burns, Martinsville, Indiana

- *Cygnus columbianus* (also called Bewick's swan)
- Chordata/Aves
- In a regional assessment by the IUCN Red List, designated as Endangered in Europe
- This swan has plumage that is entirely white, black legs, and a black beak with a yellow spot at the base. It is known as a whistling swan due to characteristic whistling in the wings.
- They nest in the Arctic tundra, then migrate to Europe and the US in the winter; their habitat is lakes, large rivers, bays, estuaries, and flooded fields.

- They are at risk because of loss of wetland habitats, changes in climate and land use, and the threat of oil development in the Arctic refuge, as well as lead poisoning from spent shot, fishing sinkers, and mine wastes deposited in sediments. Arctic breeding is in peril because of oil and gas exploration. Poaching, hunting, and avian influenza take a toll on populations.
- Some breeding areas and stopover sites are now protected as nature reserves. Conservation is sought for coastal inlets and wetlands. Reduce illegal shooting. These birds are protected under the Migratory Bird Act.

Joyce L. Carrier, Bluemont, Virginia

ULTRAMARINE LORIKEET

- *Vini ultramarine*
- Chordata/Aves
- Critically Endangered: population trend stable
- This bird is distinctive because it has orange feet and bill, and the feathers are ultramarine blue and white.
- Found on one single island in French Polynesia, Ua Huka, in the chain of Marquesas Islands in the South Pacific Ocean.
- Due to severe deforestation, fire, overgrazing, and predation of the invasive black rat, which was introduced to the islands in the 1920s, this bird is in trouble.
- The World Parrot Trust set up a grant to study the birds. Feasibility of eradication of the rat population is being examined. Local communities are being educated on ways to maintain the bird population.

David M. Taylor, Henniker, New Hampshire

Vancouver Island Marmot

- *Marmota vancouverensis*
- Chordata/Mammalia
- Critically Endangered: population decreasing
- This squirrel-like herbivore is brown with white patches. It lives in underground colonies. They weigh 6 to 15 pounds and are just over 2 feet from the tip of their nose to the tip of the tail. They hibernate in the winter, for about 210 days a year.
- Endemic to Vancouver Island, British Columbia
- This species prefers to live in meadows. In fact, when logging has occurred in an area, that is perfect habitat for the marmot. When reforestation occurs, there is steep population decline. Unlike other endangered species, reforestation puts this species in peril. Another reason the population is declining is the rise in native predators, especially cougars, wolves, and eagles. Climate change is having an adverse effect.
- To bolster populations, captive breeding programs are in the works. Protection is needed in areas with established colonies, and scientists need to continue to research their life cycle and survival needs to try to find more solutions.

VIRGINIA BIG-EARED BAT

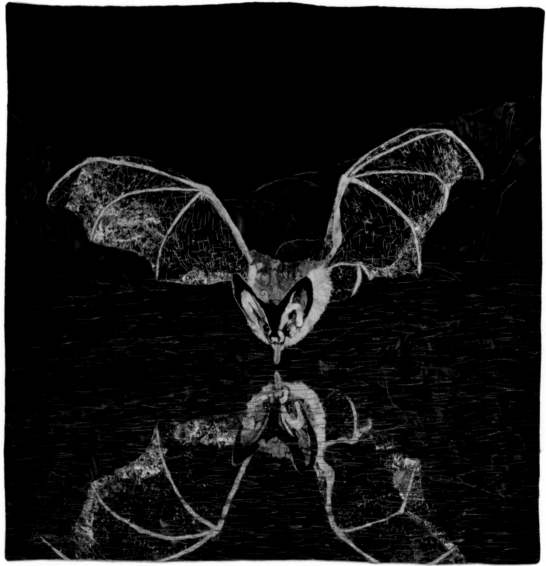

Anna Willard, Oak Hill, Virginia

- *Corynorhinus townsendii* subsp. *virginianus*
- Chordata/Mammalia
- IUCN lists these as of least concern; subspecies designated by ESA as federally and state Endangered.
- This medium-sized brown bat is 3.5 to 4 inches long and weighs less than half an ounce. The wingspan is 12 inches. It has ears more than an inch long, which are considered large compared to the overall size, and two large glands are on its muzzle. They eat mostly moths and insects, using sonar to locate them. A young bat is called a pup. This nonmigratory species has a life span of 16 years.
- Located in forest habitats in Virginia, North Carolina, Kentucky, and West Virginia. They are endemic to limestone caves.
- They are at risk due to loss of habitat. These light sleepers are easily disturbed, and humans cause them stress. White-nose syndrome is also a problem.
- To conserve the species, limit access to caves where they roost, and preserve their forest habitat. Humans should take care not to disturb bats.

VIRGINIA SNEEZEWEED

Karen Spencer Womack, Woodstock, Virginia

- *Helenium virginicum*
- Plantae/Asteraceae family
- Not evaluated by the IUCN Red List; listed as Vulnerable by NatureServe
- This rare perennial wildflower grows to a height of 3.5 feet. It is a wetland plant that grows in poorly drained, acidic loamy soil.
- Found on the western edge of the Blue Ridge Mountains, in the Shenandoah River valley of Virginia

- They are at risk because of residential development, off-road vehicle use, incompatible agricultural practices, logging, and loss of wetlands.
- To revive the species, protect ponds and enhance water quality and quantity in wetlands. Careful residential planning is necessary; increase nutrients in ponds. Do not remove plants.

Holly Cole, Triangle, Virginia

WEST AFRICAN OSTRICH

- *Struthio camelus spatzi*
- Chordata/Aves
- Endangered, according to the CITES appendix and USFWS
- The ostrich is the largest living bird in the world. They weigh an average of 285 pounds and are around 6.5 feet tall. Their long neck and long legs make them the fastest birds on land; they can run 40 miles an hour. These vegetarian birds prefer to live alone. They can survive long periods without water.
- They are found in central and southern Africa and prefer semiarid plains and woodlands.
- Ostriches are in danger because human development and agriculture are affecting their habitat. Poachers are a problem; these creatures are hunted and farmed for their feathers, skin, meat, eggs, and fat. As flightless birds, they face a wide variety of predators throughout their life cycle.
- Help may be offered in the form of donations to the African Wildlife Foundation, which works with local communities to develop plans for guiding tourism to areas not frequented by these ostriches. Efforts are being made to stabilize the remaining population.

Susan M. Bynum, Falls Church, Virginia

- *Gorilla gorilla*
- Chordata/Mammalia
- Critically Endangered: population trend decreasing
- These gorillas have black fur and large, wide skulls; their brow ridge is pronounced and they have small ears. Their legs are shorter than their arms, and they walk on their knuckles. The males weigh between 300 and 500 pounds, they are 6 feet tall, and their arm span is approximately 8 feet. Females are 4.5 feet tall and weigh 150 to 200 pounds. Communication with one another is via auditory signals, visual signals, and odors. They are mostly herbivores, and they live in small groups of five to eight animals. In the wild they can live 30 to 40 years.
- They live in the Congo Basin, which spans Cameroon, Central Africa Republic, Democratic Republic of the Congo, Republic of the Congo, Equatorial Guinea, and Gabon. The Congo basin habitat includes rivers, forests, savannas, swamps, and flooded forests.
- Reasons for their decline include loss of habitat due to logging, disease (including Ebola), and poaching.
- Conservation efforts should focus on strengthening protected areas, gorilla tracking programs, promoting sustainable development, and research to adapt the human Ebola vaccine to save gorillas.

Western Prairie Fringed Orchid

Suzanne Meader, Sterling, Virginia

- *Platanthera praeclara*
- Plantae/Orchidaceae family
- Endangered: population decreasing
- A perennial plant that thrives in sun, moist prairies, and calcareous meadows. They grow 16 to 36 inches tall and have creamy white, heavily fringed flowers. The stem is smooth, and pointed leaves start at the base and get smaller toward the top, where the flower blooms. They grow among tall prairie grasses.
- Located west of the Mississippi River, in Iowa, Kansas, Minnesota, Missouri, Nebraska, North Dakota, Oklahoma, and Manitoba, Canada

- These plants are at risk because of conversion of pastures and hayfields to croplands, reduced soil moisture, ditching, irrigation systems, and herbicides and insecticides, which jeopardize survival of necessary pollinators.
- A federal recovery plan by the USFWS is underway. State laws restrict projects that would impact the species on public lands, and some states restrict taking the plant from public lands for sale, trade, or export. Permits are required for collection for international trade and export. Strict penalties for violation include a fine of up to $50,000 or one year in jail.

Starla Phelps, Alexandria, Virginia

- *Chelonoidis porteri*
- Chordata/Reptilia
- Critically Endangered: population trend increasing
- Galápagos tortoises grow to 6 feet and weigh more than 500 pounds, making them the largest in the world. They continue to grow until they are 40 to 50 years old; many survive to be 100. This superpower makes them the longest living of all vertebrates. These cold-blooded animals have thick legs and a dome-shaped shell; they rest approximately 16 hours a day. Their massive shell is not solid; it is made up of plates and contains the ribs of the animal. As a result, the tortoise is unable to walk out of their shell. It is made up of something like honeycombs, which have small air chambers. There is a hissing sound when it pulls itself into its shell, because the lungs are located at the top of the body, and the hiss is air being released. They eat slowly but can consume 80 pounds of food a day, and they drink enormous amounts of water. Another of their superpowers is a slow metabolism that allows them to survive a year without food or water when necessary.
- Found on the western side of the island of Santa Cruz in the Galápagos
- Habitat destruction and illegal hunting for shells and eggs are the main threats. Hawks are the only native predator for the eggs and tortoise hatchlings. Invasive predators are a major threat, especially feral pigs.
- Galápagos National Park was established to protect tortoises. In 1969, the Charles Darwin Research Station received funding from the San Diego Zoo for a tortoise-rearing facility. This site provides a head start to hatchlings by raising them until they can survive on their own, thus avoiding predators. The success rate in hatching in captivity has reached 75 percent. Workshops and studies are sponsored that foster and implement more constructive ideas. It is illegal to hunt or capture the tortoises.

Lynn Chinnis, Oro Valley, Arizona

- *Charadrius alexandrinus nivosis*
- Chordata/Aves
- Threatened, according to the US Fish & Wildlife Service
- This shorebird, with a white belly, tan topside, and black markings near the throat, nests on beaches above the high-tide line, in sparsely vegetated dunes.
- Located in Washington, Oregon, California, and Mexico

- Human activity on beaches, the growth of nonnative grasses, and development are leading to a loss of nesting sites. Eggs deposited in shallow sand depressions are affected by the weather.
- Limiting vehicles and horses on beaches, roping off nesting areas, eradicating nonnative grasses, and closing beaches during nesting season all are efforts toward conservation.

WHALE SHARK

Linda P. Keithley, Centreville, Virginia

- *Rincodon typus*
- Chordata/Chondrichthyes
- Endangered: population decreasing
- This shark grows to 40 feet in length, making it the largest living fish in the world. Its back is gray with unique patterns of white spots that vary in intensity and number over the length of the body. The underside is white. They are filter feeders and eat plankton and small fish.
- They are found in the warm waters of the Atlantic Ocean and the Indo-Pacific Ocean.
- Asian menus specialize in shark fin soup, which puts this species in peril. The meat, oil, and fins are prized by unregulated fisheries.
- To bring back this species, we need to teach people about the life cycle, migratory patterns, reproduction, and habitat of the whale shark. Laws must be passed prohibiting the sale of products containing their meat and fins. Protect and conserve the oceans. Educate tourists.

WHITE-BELLIED HERON

Priscilla Stultz, Williamsburg, Virginia

- *Ardea insignis* (also commonly called the imperial heron)
- Chordata/Aves
- Critically Endangered: population trend decreasing
- These are large herons, approximately 50 inches tall and 4 to 6 pounds, with a 6.5-foot wingspan. They are darkish gray brown, with contrasting white on various areas of the body, and are mostly solitary. They use a large, pointed beak to spear their food, mostly fish and insects. When disturbed they make a deep croaking noise. They breed and nest in trees.

- The few remaining heron are located in India, Bhutan, Bangladesh, and Myanmar. Their habitat is marsh and wetlands, on riverbanks.
- Reasons for the decline in numbers include wetlands degradation, human disturbance, pollution, and poaching (eggs are also poached). Hydroelectric dams near their breeding grounds and road improvements are having an adverse effect.
- Breeding programs in reserves, wildlife sanctuaries in India, protection by the Royal Society for Protection of Nature, tagging of the birds, and training "heron guardians" where they are found—all are measures to try to revive the species.

Jeanie Sakrison Velarde, Cordova, Tennessee

WHOOPING CRANE

- *Grus americana*
- Chordata/Aves
- Endangered: population trend increasing
- Nicknamed "whoopers," the Audubon Society calls this bird one of the most magnificent in all of North America. Standing as tall as 5 feet, they have a 7.5-foot wingspan and weigh up to 16 pounds. White with a red crown and a long, dark bill, these are omnivores (animals eating both plants and animals) that nest on marshy ground. Their superpower is a loud, trumpetlike call, heard for several miles, which is used upon waking as a warning and to defend their territory, and as part of the courtship ritual. Predators are many: bear, wolverines, wolves, mountain lions, fox, lynx, eagles, ravens, bobcats, and alligators. Their life span is 22 to 24 years.
- Located in Wood Buffalo National Park in Alberta, Canada, and at Aransas National Wildlife Refuge on the Gulf coast of Texas
- They are in jeopardy because of habitat loss and hunting.
- David Sakrison (this quilt artist's brother), who works in the crane conservation field, has used ultralight aircraft to teach captive-reared fledgling cranes how to migrate. He says federal protection and other conservation efforts have allowed the flock in Aransas National Wildlife Refuge in Texas to grow. However, a single population is too vulnerable to natural or human-made hazards. Since 2001, Operation Migration (OM) and the Eastern Whooping Crane Partnership have been creating a new, separate migratory flock east of the Mississippi by introducing captive-raised chicks into the wild. Operation Migration continues to monitor the flock and to introduce new chicks directly into that population. These numbers remain very small, however, and the species remains extremely vulnerable. Whoopers reproduce slowly, and predation, illegal hunting, and threats to their habitat continue to thwart recovery efforts. There is hope that the haunting calls of this majestic and iconic bird will not be lost to the ages, thanks to the continued efforts of OM, the International Crane Foundation, and other partners.

Joanne Strehle Bast, Littlestown, Pennsylvania

WILD WATER BUFFALO

- *Bubalus arnee*
- Chordata/Mammalia
- Endangered: population decreasing
- Among the heaviest stocky, shorter-legged bovid species (59–75 inches at shoulder height, 94–118 inches in length, 1,300–2,600 pounds), both sexes have scimitar-shaped horns (up to 79 inches across), a tufted forehead, and long, coarse hair.
- Wetlands habitat is located in parts of Nepal, Bhutan, Thailand, Cambodia, Myanmar, India, and Madhya Pradesh.
- Endangered due to poaching for their horns, loss of habitat, interbreeding with feral and domestic buffalo, and competition for food and water with other animals
- To recover the species, it is necessary to protect their habitats, remove domestic animals from wild habitats, and eliminate poaching.

WOODCHAT SHRIKE

Sarah Lykins Entsminger, Ashburn, Virginia

- *Lanius senator*
- Chordata/Aves
- Listed by IUCN as least concern, with declining populations, but designated Critically Endangered on the Red List in Switzerland
- The male is described as a striking bird with black-and-white plumage and a chestnut head. A fully migratory bird, they spend winters in tropical Africa, then return through the Mediterranean (mainly in Spain) and breed in Europe. During breeding season they prefer semiopen areas such as woodlands, old orchards, vineyards, and gardens. They eat insects and small vertebrates. These birds are 6 to 10 inches long and possess strong legs, sharp claws, and a hooked bill with a tooth behind the hook.
- Found in Europe, the Middle East, and Africa

- These birds have almost completely disappeared from their breeding grounds in Switzerland. The primary cause is destruction and alteration of habitat caused in part by the use of agrochemicals, hunting, and human interference. Climate change is playing a detrimental role.
- This species is legally protected in Switzerland. Other steps for conservation include prevention of hunting, tight control of herbicides and insecticides, and soil rotation practices. It would be advantageous to leave areas unplowed around field margins. A return to traditional management of pastoral woodland and livestock rearing would be helpful. Consider leaving old-growth trees along the edges of vineyards, and encourage protection of old-growth orchards.

Yellow Teardrop Butterflyfish

Dianne Harris Thomas, Fairfax, Virginia

- *Chaetodon unimaculatus*
- Chordata/Actinopterygii
- Although listed as of least concern on the IUCN Red List, according to an April 16, 2018, article on https://a-z-animals.com, the butterfly fish is Endangered.
- These fish are bright yellow with a black "eyespot," and they have a black vertical stripe through their eye. They have a rounded, flat shape and feed on plankton, sea urchins, algae, and coral. They grow to nearly 8 inches long and have an eight-to-ten-year life span.
- They live in the West Indian Ocean from South Africa to Sumatra, among coral and in rocky areas off the coast. They travel in groups when feeding and are hunted by eels, snappers, grouper, barracuda, and shark.
- Populations are at risk because of degradation of coral reefs, water pollution, habitat loss, and collection by saltwater enthusiasts.
- Health must be restored to coral reefs. Regulate collection and make commercial sale illegal.

ON MAMMALS AND REVIVING SPECIES

Janet Rachlow and Jim Witham

Mammals are found worldwide; they inhabit all continents, including Antarctica (think seals), and they live in environments ranging from deserts to ice sheets to oceans. Although several characteristics are shared among all mammals—for example, milk production and hair—the group includes an amazing diversity of form and lifestyle. Their body sizes span orders of magnitude, from a minute shrew that weighs less than a penny to the 300,000-pound blue whale, the largest mammal ever to have lived on Earth. Collectively, mammals fly, swim, burrow, run, glide, hop, and climb trees, and while doing so, they exhibit complex social and individual behaviors that allow them to thrive in their natural environments. There is a lot to love about these animals!

Mammals are classified into three main types that are based on their pattern of reproduction. We think of placental mammals, more correctly called eutherian mammals, as the "regular type" that gives birth to relatively well-developed young. In contrast, marsupial mammals such as opossums and kangaroos have tiny young that complete much of their fetal development outside the mother's body, often in a pouch on her belly. Even stranger are the handful of mammal species in the third group, the monotremes, which exhibit the most primitive mode of reproduction, laying soft-shelled eggs that hatch into baby mammals after a few weeks; these include the duck-billed platypus and several species of echidna.

So, how many species of mammals are there on Earth today? Like so many simple questions, this one is challenging to answer. We know that some mammals have become extinct in the past couple of centuries. One of the most recent is a rodent that lived on an island in the Great Barrier Reef of Australia. Rising ocean levels reduced the island size, and salt water from high tides killed island vegetation; this is the first mammal extinction attributed to climate change. Fortunately, however, the number of known extinctions is still relatively

small (about 1.5 percent of living mammals or an estimated 96 species in the past 500 years). And in fact, the estimated number of mammal species has increased each year for several reasons. First, new species are still being discovered, and not just rats and bats, but even large mammals! A few years ago, a new carnivore about the size of a house cat, the olinguito, was discovered in a museum collection; the specimen had been misidentified for decades. The scientists who realized this mistake returned to Ecuador, where the animal was originally collected, and found living olinguitos in the trees! In the past few decades, other exciting discoveries have included new species of monkeys in South America and Africa, whales, and even large, deerlike animals in Asia. Another reason that the known number of mammals increases each year is that we have more refined methods to identify species, and sometimes what was thought to be a single species in fact represents two or more distinct ones. The number of mammals on Earth now is estimated to be around 6,400, although this number will continue to change. A great place to explore up-to-date information on mammals is the Mammal Diversity Database website (https://mammaldiversity.org), created by the American Society of Mammalogists.

Even though the number of known mammal species is increasing, roughly 20 percent of mammals worldwide are categorized as endangered or threatened on the basis of global assessments conducted by the IUCN. Loss and modification of their habitats are the primary causes of endangerment, and for marine mammals, threats include harvest, pollution, and strikes by sea vessels in shipping lanes. Degraded and fragmented habitats often support fewer individuals within smaller areas, and these factors set the stage for species sliding down the slippery slope toward small population size and, ultimately, extinction.

Although some mammals have become extinct, many have been brought back from the brink of extinction. Several of these species are illustrated in this volume: the southern white rhinoceros (the northern subspecies is pictured on page 154), elk (page 258), bison (page 254), and the Columbia Basin pygmy rabbit (page 256). These examples illustrate how dedication, focused efforts, adequate funding, available habitat, and a little luck can help reverse population declines; however, the most successful and economical approach is to prevent numbers from getting so low that a species becomes a candidate for endangered status.

Mammals are probably the best-studied group of animals, but there is still so much to learn about them. My graduate students and I have been studying pygmy rabbits for almost two decades, and each year there have been surprising discoveries. For example, one discovery important to management and conservation resulted from using tiny radiotelemetry tags glued onto the backs of two-to-four-week-old juveniles. We learned that young rabbits can disperse much, much farther than anyone guessed. The record in our study went to a seven-week-old female that traveled over 7 miles in about a week before settling into a new area. This is good news for the species because it means that populations that are separated can potentially exchange individuals, boosting genetic diversity and increasing the probability of persistence over time. Learning more about the ecology and lives of animals is not only interesting but provides information that can help managers plan for their conservation.

We are sometimes asked why conservation of endangered species is important. There are many ways to think about this question that evoke ethics, aesthetics, or human well-being. In our view, one of the most persuasive arguments for conserving wild plants and animals is that parts of the natural world interact in ways that we have yet to learn or even imagine. The renowned conservationist Aldo Leopold wrote, "To keep every cog and wheel is the first precaution of intelligent tinkering." One thing that we learned about pygmy rabbits helps illustrate this point. Pygmy rabbits not only eat sagebrush shrubs, but they do much to "farm" them. The rabbits' fecal pellets accumulate and decompose around their burrows, nourishing the surrounding plants, and their digging creates areas of soft soil where sagebrush seedlings flourish. There are numerous other examples of how animals interact with the environment in positive ways, and how losing one piece of the puzzle can have cascading secondary consequences.

There are important ways that we all can help promote conservation and our coexistence with wildlife. First, be an enthusiastic and vocal ambassador for conservation. The old saying that we will preserve only what we love is true. Sharing a genuine passion for animals and their natural habitats helps others connect more deeply with the natural world. This seems especially important in this time of advanced technology, which isolates us almost as much as connecting us together.

Second, we all make daily personal decisions about how we choose to use limited resources, and doing so thoughtfully can help reduce our individual impact on the environment.

Finally, actively seek current and accurate information about global conservation issues and energetically support local efforts to promote conservation of natural resources, including endangered species. Everything each of us does has a positive and cumulative effect on our communities.

We were once kids, and our world has changed greatly during our lifetimes. Almost all kids are fascinated with animals, especially mammals, and we found ways to live out that fascination. We both have been fortunate to have had careers that allowed us to study wild mammals, including rhinos, bears, bighorn sheep, coyotes, and, more recently, pygmy rabbits. Janet is a professor of wildlife ecology at the University of Idaho, and although Jim is retired after serving as a biologist at multiple state wildlife agencies, we enjoy working together on research and sharing our enthusiasm for the natural world with others.

Janet Rachlow
Professor, Department of Fish and Wildlife Sciences, University of Idaho

Jim Witham
Retired wildlife biologist

June 23, 2018

Cheryl Rounds, Vienna, Virginia

SUCCESS STORY #1:
AMERICAN BISON

- *Bison bison*
- Chordata/Mammalia
- Near Threatened: population stable
- This large animal, dark brown with long shaggy hair on the front legs, is 5 to 6 feet tall and weighs 800 to 2,000 pounds. It has a large head and curved horns that can be 2 feet long. Their life span is 12 to 20 years. These herbivores eat grass and plants and travel in herds. They can run 40 miles per hour. Did you know that a bison is not the same as a buffalo? They belong to the same family, but there are some critical differences. Buffalo species do not have a beard, and they live in Africa and Asia. Bison have beards, and they are native to North and South America and Europe.
- Located at Yellowstone National Park, in Utah and South Dakota, and in Alberta and the southern part of the Northwest Territories in Canada, and a few other national parks and other small wildlife areas
- Unregulated hunting and interbreeding with cattle puts them at risk.
- Conservation efforts by private landowners and state and federal agencies helped rebuild herds by protecting and providing open grasslands. Agencies are trying a new approach, focusing on managing the genetics, to prevent "genomic extinction" through hybridization.

Etta McFarland, Olive Branch, Mississippi

SUCCESS STORY #2:
COLUMBIA BASIN PYGMY RABBIT

- *Brachylagus idahoensis*
- Chordata/Mammalia
- IUCN Red List classifies this as of least concern; USFWS and USDA determined it is Endangered: the population is increasing.
- About the size of a kitten, these are the smallest rabbits in North America. They are the only North American rabbits that live in a sagebrush habitat where they dig their own burrows. They eat sagebrush almost exclusively in the winter.
- Found in the Sagebrush Flats Wildlife Area in the Columbia Basin region of Washington State
- For thousands of years their population has been isolated, and inbreeding became a problem. Over the last 160 years, sagebrush-covered lands have been converted for agricultural purposes to improve livestock forage, so habitat and food sources have been lost. Other factors such as disease, wildfire, and predation have reduced numbers.
- In 2002, the Oregon Zoo, in cooperation with the Washington Department of Fish and Wildlife, the USFWS, and Washington State University, removed the last 16 pygmy rabbits from their natural habitat and started a 12-year breeding program. They crossbred these rabbits with pygmy rabbits from Idaho. Nine years into that program, pygmy rabbits that had been bred in captivity were reintroduced into small, protected areas within their natural wildlife area, where they are closely monitored. In 2011, for the first time in more than a decade, pygmy rabbits bred and gave birth in the wild. These results are encouraging; with continued close monitoring, there is hope that this rabbit population will thrive in their natural habitat.

Laura Catherine Gilmartin, Stafford, Virginia

Success Story #3:
Elk

- *Cervus canadensis*
- Chordata/Mammalia
- Designated least concern: population trend increasing
- Male bull elk weigh approximately 700 pounds and are 5 feet tall, shoulder height. Females weigh closer to 500 pounds, and they are slightly shorter. Calves weigh approximately 30 pounds at birth. They feed on grasses, sedges and other herbs and shrubs, bark of aspen trees, conifer needles, burned bark, and aquatic plants. Their life span is 10 to 13 years.
- Before European settlement, an estimated ten million elk roamed throughout what is now the US and parts of Canada. Elk adapted to almost all ecosystems except for the tundra, true deserts, and the Gulf coast. Today, about one million elk live in the western, central, and eastern US and from Ontario into western Canada.
- Elk were considered endangered in the 1930s due to overhunting. Western expansion, trophy hunting, and development pushed them into the mountainous terrain of the western Rocky Mountain states and the Pacific Northwest.
- As herds diminished, men such as Teddy Roosevelt saw the need to start a conservation movement to help protect some of the dwindling elk herds and other animals that were hunted to near extinction. States enacted hunting regulations and outlawed market hunting. Sanctuaries such as Yellowstone National Park were established, and elk were slowly reintroduced to areas where they had been extirpated. From a low of 50,000 total elk to the current estimates of around one million elk in North America, elk have proven to be adaptive and resilient. Kentucky, Kansas, Nebraska, North Carolina, Michigan, Missouri, Minnesota, Pennsylvania, and Wisconsin all have initiated programs to transplant or rebuild elk herds. The Rocky Mountain Elk Foundation (RMEF), a conservation organization based in Montana whose stated mission is "to ensure the future of elk, other wildlife, their habitat and our hunting heritage," has teamed with the game and fish departments of various states to relocate elk from areas in the West. The RMEF has provided money for habitat development and land acquisition in states with viable elk populations. The number of elk that have rebounded is evidence that conservation can save a species.

Anna Willard, Oak Hill, Virginia

SUCCESS STORY #4:
KIRTLAND'S WARBLER

- *Setophaga kirtlandii*
- Chordata/Aves
- Near Threatened; listed by USFWS as Endangered: population trend increasing
- This is a small, blue-gray bird with a yellow chest. They nest in jack pine trees in branches close to the ground and need a thickly forested area to breed. Their diet consists mostly of insects, grubs, and blueberries.
- Habitat is in Ontario, Michigan, and Wisconsin; they migrate to the Bahamas for the winter season.
- Originally endangered because the jack pines they breed in require forest fires to open their pine cones and disperse seeds for new trees. Wildfires ceased for a time, and new growth was halted. Once controlled wildfires were introduced, new growth of these trees began, and the species is recovering. Another problem is that cowbirds were laying eggs in warbler nests. The warblers would then raise those nestlings. Cowbird removal has helped tremendously.
- One of the very first species to be listed as endangered, with approximately only 160 birds remaining, this warbler is an example of a tremendous conservation success story. Thanks to efforts of state and federal agencies and conservation groups, trees they depend on are plentiful, the problematic cowbird population has been reduced, and the warblers are thriving.

ART AND HEART:
OUR PLACE IN THE STORY

Vance Martin

A picture is worth a thousand words. Images of wildlife captured by cameras are as heartwarming and interesting as they can be informative.

As interesting and important as the photographs are, however, wildlife images actually created by human hands are to my mind worth even more because they are timeless, and part of an iconic tradition that dates to the earliest humans. From ancient to modern times, the depiction of wildlife has been an integral and constant aspect of human history and evolution. Human-drawn wildlife figures, the very earliest form of artistic expression, are almost always found on rock panels and cave walls, many of which were associated with primitive human figures. Like all true art, such images convey emotion, skill, and culture. They tell a story of relationship: of artist to subject, and human society to nature.

The cave paintings of Lascaux in southern France, some 20,000 years old, show the ancient aurochs, a wild bovine that shaped the mosaic of forest and meadow that was for eons the landscape of primeval Europe. The aurochs exists no more, extinct because of the impact of humans on the species and the landscape.

In Niger, West Africa, giraffes are painted onto rock boulders in the Sahel, on the fringes of the Sahara Desert, where the giraffe no longer exists; some of these are the largest pictographs in the world. Estimated at 8,000 years old, these tell stories of human art and heart. They record a landscape drastically altered from abundant grassland and tree-dotted savanna to desert sand and scrub, the result of changes in climate caused in part by human use of land that altered habitat and ecological processes.

Then there are the more than 5,000-year-old figures of desert bighorn sheep and antelope that adorn rocky overhangs and rock stacks in the Utah Canyonlands. These pictographs reveal a reverence and respect for animals that shared the land with and brought everything to the Anasazi people: relationship, worship, food, tools, and clothing.

The rock faces of Huangushu in central China (and elsewhere) are often painted with human torsos that have animal heads, antlers, or cloven hooves (or a mix of these). They speak to us of the animistic bonding and spiritual coexistence of humankind and animals.

On isolated "erratic" boulders in northern Scandinavia, one sees caribou being herded into primitive fenced enclosures, telling us the story of early domestication of wild nature. This was the emergence of the reindeer culture among the Saami people that occurred within the Intel peoples of Kamchatka and their many ethnic kin and neighbors across the boreal North.

There is the continual growth in style and expression of "wildlife art" as diverse as the oil masterpieces of Rungius and Liljefors; the contemporary work of many such as Robert Bateman, James Fiorentino, David Shepherd, Simon Combes; female artists Sandy Scott, Tran Nguyen, Rosa Bonheur, Joan Monroe, and the fabulous late Lanford Monroe; the pop-art posters of Andy Warhol; the duck stamps of the US Postal Service; the wildlife fetishes of the Zuni and other Pueblo people; and the sculptures of Sandy Scott, Bob Kuhn, Terry Matthews . . . and so many more.

Such is the tradition, the continuum, of artistic depiction of the relationship between humans and wildlife in which reside the artists of this lovely volume of work you have in your hands. This noble, ancient, revered, and enjoyable genre is as important today as it was to the hunters, shamans, and artists of prehistory. But I suggest to you that the role of the fiber artists in this wonderful compendium of contemporary quilts is perhaps even more important than that of their predecessors. This is because the human-nature relationship is at a crossroads today, one characterized by environmental macrochange not experienced by the ancient artists or their successors.

The artists in this book are doing far more than practicing their craft, hobby, or profession. They bear witness to what is now referred to as the Sixth Great Extinction crisis. This is a planetary-scale phenomenon accelerated by the impacts of human activities and technologies that are generating systemic climate change, extensive habitat conversion and destruction, and pervasive toxicity. In the understandable drive to create human safety and well-being, we have created a society divorced from our wild roots, disassociated from the wilderness in which we evolved, and alienated from the natural processes generated by wilderness that are still needed today to support all life on Earth. This is what most people refer to as progress.

Animals, especially wildlife, are our brothers. Our fascination with them, perhaps more than anything else on Earth, demonstrated by wildlife being the oldest and most continuous subject of human artwork, is because they mirror us. When we look at them we see part of ourselves. Even more, they subconsciously remind us of a mystery we have forgotten, and a heritage we ignore at our own peril.

I hope you have enjoyed this fine and wonderful book. From whimsy to wildness, it depicts an important ancient tradition and modern reality. Thank the artists. Bless the animals. And be moved to act on behalf of wildlife and wilderness—it is never too late.

Vance G. Martin
President, the WILD Foundation; and Wilderness Foundation global founder-cochair, Wilderness Specialist Group, World Commission on Protected Areas / IUCN

Information about the Quilts

All the quilts in this book are 24 inches by 24 inches, consisting of at least three layers (a front, middle, and back) and stitching. They each have a sleeve on the back to facilitate hanging in exhibits. The exhibit premieres at the Houston International Quilt Festival, which is the largest quilt show in the world, in the fall of 2019.

Acalypha wigginsii: Cotton fabric, yarn. Cathron knitted the flowers. Machine appliquéd and machine quilted.

addax: Cotton, leather, suede, vinyl, and fleece. The antlers were stuffed with batting, and parts were sewn with elastic thread so the puckering effect would imitate ridges in the antlers. From left to right, the antlers get lighter to show these animals fading away.

African elephant: Hand-dyed cotton fabrics, sheer overlay, ribbon, feathers. Raw-edge appliquéd and machine quilted, embellished.

African lion: Cotton fabric, alpaca wool, wool roving, Tsukineko® inks, Derwent® Inktense Pencils. Painted, layered, machine stitched, thread painted, hand embellished. Laura says her biggest challenge was to make the eyes look real and to convey fierceness.

African wild dog: Cotton fabrics, acrylic paint, and watercolor pencils. Raw-edge appliquéd, collaged and layered, machine quilted. Teresa uses at least one new technique whenever she participates in a challenge. The photo, used with permission for inspiration, was taken by wildlife photographer Gerry van der Walt of Wild Eye Destinations.

Aleutian shield fern: Cotton fabric. Fern fronds were created separately with black batting in the middle, then were cut apart and machine appliquéd to the machine-quilted background. The stitched drawing of the fern is the actual size of the plant, while the quilted version is greatly enlarged. Nancy lived in Alaska for nearly five years with her husband, who was in the military. This gave her a special appreciation for plants and animals that can survive the challenges of a harsh environment. A tiny fern clinging to a crack in the rocks was the perfect subject.

American bison: Cotton fabric, fusible web. Cheryl used Susan Carlson's method of fabric collage and fusible appliqué. To her, bison represent strength, independence, pride, and rulers of the Plains; they are an important symbol of Native American culture. Seeing a free-roaming bison was pure delight.

Amur leopard: Commercial cotton, hand-dyed fabric, nylon netting, tulle. Fabric collaged, raw-edge appliquéd, machine quilted. Ricki works best when she connects emotionally with her subject. She spent a day working on the eyes of the leopard, hoping they will help others connect emotionally. She desperately hopes that through her art, she can inspire awareness and love for this species and that this love will translate into action and advocacy. Valerie Abbott generously collaborated on this project by taking the photo Ricki worked from. Susan Carlson taught this method of fabric collage.

Andean flamingo: Various cotton fabrics and glittery metallic thread. Sketched, raw-edge appliquéd, fabric collaged, machine quilted, and topstitched.

arroyo toad: Cotton fabric, tulle, beads. Confetti collaged, hand appliquéd, machine pieced, machine quilted, embellished. Thanks to Gary Nafis of California Herps, whose photography inspired this quilt. The arroyo toads live in Karen's county; she hopes they make a comeback.

Asiatic black bear: Cotton fabric, wool and velvet, seed beads. The background was designed with traditional "bear paw" quilt blocks; appliquéd and hand stitched, embellished.

Asiatic lion: Cotton fabric, alpaca wool, wool roving, Tsukineko® inks, Derwent® Inktense Pencils, yarns, and Seta paints. Painted background, thread painted, appliquéd, couched. Nashad Abdu (https://unsplash.com) gave permission to use his photos as inspiration.

Atlantic bluefin tuna: Cotton and synthetic fabric. English paper pieced, machine pieced, hand and machine appliquéd, machine quilted.

Atlantic sturgeon: Hand-dyed fabric, cotton quilting fabric. Hand pieced, hand appliquéd, hand quilted. Permission granted from Bethanne Nemesh to use her jellyfish quilting designs.

Attenborough's long-beaked echidna: Cotton and upholstery fabric, fake fur, Texture Magic®, embroidery thread, yarn, fusible web. Drawn, fused, embellished, raw-edge appliquéd, and machine quilted.

bactrian camel: Cotton fabric, Jacquard™ textile color, Inktense colored pencils. Drawn, painted, machine quilted, thread painted, colored. Techniques used are briefly explored in Barbara's book *Quilting with Doilies: Inspiration, Techniques and Projects* (Atglen, PA: Schiffer, 2015).

Baker's larkspur: Cotton fabric, watercolor pencils, fabric paint. Hand pieced and hand appliquéd, painted, hand quilted. Photographer Vernon Smith sent Sandi photos as inspiration and an article on this larkspur written by his wife, Doreen Smith. Aaron Arthur, another photographer, shared his photos for further inspiration.

black rhinoceros: Cotton fabrics and batiks, fusible web, commercial and hand-dyed rickrack. Raw-edge machine appliquéd. Vanessa took a photo for this quilt at the American Museum of Natural History in Manhattan, where there is a beautiful black rhinoceros diorama (www.amnh.org/exhibitions/permanent-exhibitions/mammal-halls/akeley-hall-of-african-mammals/black-rhinoceros). "How sad if the only place my grandson can see these wonderful beasts is stuffed by the taxidermist in museum dioramas." She credits Wendy Richardson of the Quilt Tapestry Studio, who dyed the rickrack.

black-capped vireo: Batik and quilting cottons, fusible web, various threads. Sandy started with a simplified drawing by her sister Bonnie Adams of McBain, Michigan, on the basis of a photograph credited to Alan Schmierer (www.flickr.com/photos/sloalan/), which he generously licensed as Creative Commons public domain. The photo was used for color suggestions and as a guide for contrast. Raw-edge appliquéd, machine quilted. Sandy taught endangered species in middle school science. She discovered that this vireo is native to an area she explored in Oklahoma's Wichita Mountains National Wildlife Refuge. She remembers the buffalo, elk, and rattlesnakes, but this bird is often heard and rarely seen.

black-footed ferret: Cotton fabric, various threads, Pellon Fabric Magic, glass and stone beads, colored pencils, Inktense pencils, fabric medium, acrylic paint. Drawn, free-motion embroidered, machine appliquéd, colored, painted, embroidered, and beaded. Kimberly Fraser, US Fish & Wildlife Service, Mountain Prairie Region, posted a photo to their Flickr feed that Barbara obtained permission to use as inspiration. Thanks to Joyce Hughes for a class on thread painting, and to Linda Poole for instruction and inspiration in painted appliqué at the Mid-Appalachian Quilters Summer 2017 Retreat.

Blackburn's sphinx moth: Burlap, batik, Pellon Peltex and other Pellon products, Dye-Na-Flow® paints, pipe cleaner, synthetic fur and yarns. Machine appliquéd, painted, free-motion quilted. Images used for inspiration were a variety of pictures from https://commons.wikimedia.org. This insect is a creature of the night, and it took careful research and planning to achieve a night scene and still keep the quilt appearance bright. This quilt shows much of the moth's life cycle. Depicted are an egg cluster, larvae feeding on the aiea leaves, and the adult moth taking flight.

blue whale: Cottons, silk, polyester, duchess satin, fabric paint. Painted, collaged and layered, machine appliquéd. Some techniques were learned online from video tutorials. Pascale credits Beth Uda of Zazu's Stitch Art (www.zazusstitchart.com/zazus-tutorials/).

blue-throated macaw: Cotton fabric, Inktense pens, Tsukineko® inks, feathers, glue, plastic, shimmery synthetic fabric, cork fabric, tulle. Painted, hand quilted, trapunto, machine quilted, thread painted. A photo by Dario Podesta of Bolivia (www.dariopodesta.com/en/), used with permission, presented an idea to show the birds trying to nest in a dead palm tree.

bocaccio rockfish: Cotton fabric, fluid textile paint, 20/80 nonwoven wool felt, various decorative threads. Original stamp carved by artist from recycled rubber, monoprinted, machine stitched.

Bornean orangutan: Cotton fabric, alpaca wool, wool roving, Tsukineko® inks, Derwent® Inktense Pencils, cork fabric, Seta transparent paints, various threads, netting. Painted, thread painted, appliquéd, layered for dimension, machine quilted. Laura acknowledges the group that runs the sanctuary for orangutans in Borneo, the Great Projects. Connor Whelan gave her permission to use one of their photographs as inspiration. Laura says when she found this photo, she felt as if she could see into the orangutan's eyes and into his soul. Her challenge was to convey those feelings she had for him.

Bougainville moustached kingfisher: Cotton fabric. Drawn and machine appliquéd.

bridled nailtail wallaby: Cotton fabrics, embroidery floss, various threads, velvet rickrack. Drawn, machine appliquéd, hand embroidered, machine quilted. A map of Australia and special Australian fabrics were incorporated into this quilt. Special thanks to Steve Parish (www.steveparish-natureconnect.com.au) for permission to use a photo for inspiration, to painting teacher Deborah Ellis for advice, and to Kate Grumbacher, who helped attach the hanging sleeve on the back.

buffy-headed marmoset: Cotton fabrics and wool roving. Freezer paper machine pieced, machine quilted, needle felted.

burrowing owl: Batiks and hand-dyed fabrics by Wendy Richardson, fusible web, decorative threads. Machine appliquéd, hand embroidered, machine embroidered, machine quilted. Thanks to Claire's husband for suggesting she depict this species.

California condor: Cotton fabric, metallic and other thread, fusible web. Machine appliquéd, thread painted. The raw-edge appliqué method and thread painting were learned from teacher Susan Carlson. Karen thought most artists would make cute quilts of endangered species for this project. She says this ugly bird needed a spot in the book. Since she sees many vultures in her own backyard, she has a liking for these scavengers. Thanks to Cheryl Rounds for yarn and inspiration.

Cape Sable seaside sparrow: Cotton fabric. Painted with crayons and pens, machine-pieced background, hand appliquéd and embroidered. Thanks to appliqué teachers Rose Hahn, Elly Sienkiewicz, and Mimi Dietrich. Dottie's late husband had a 35-year career with the USFWS, working his last 15 years as chief of scientific authority with CITES. He identified over 270 bird species in the field before entering college and instilled in Dottie an interest in birds.

cape seahorse: Batik fabrics, embellishments. Machine appliquéd using decorative machine stitching. A special curved ruler designed by Cheryl Lynch was used to cut the background fabric.

channel-billed toucan: Batiks, basting glue. Machine appliquéd. With permission, Sue used a photo taken by Emmanuel Keller, who calls himself Tambako the Jaguar, for inspiration. Credit is given to Susan Carlson for the technique as described in her books *Free-Style Quilts* and *Serendipity Quilts*.

cheetah: Cotton, batik, hand-painted fabric, tulle, leather piping. Sketched, Susan Carlson's fabric collage appliquéd method, machine quilted, hand embroidered. Diane grew up watching *Wild Kingdom*, loves all animals, and uses them in much of her work.

chimpanzee: Cotton sateen. Ice-dyed fabric, hand painted, free-motion quilted. Holly used anatomical studies and a copyright-free image from Pixabay for reference. She wanted to create both a palpably human feel and a sense of disappearing; she says that looking at their expressive faces and witnessing the tender care of their young makes it impossible to deny our common bonds and heritage.

Chinese alligator: Cotton fabrics, woven picot, fusible web, hand-dyed cotton string by Wendy Richardson of the Quilt Tapestry Studio, embroidery threads, plastic sequins, silver spangles, glass montee beads. Raw-edge machine appliquéd, raised embroidered, beaded, prairie points constructed, stuffed appliquéd. Vanessa's bachelor's degree is in biology; her quilt is named *Jewel of the Beautiful Yangtze River*.

Chisos Mountain hedgehog cactus: Batik fabric, fusible web, various threads. Machine appliquéd, free-motion quilted.

coelacanth: Cotton fabric, hologram thread, crystals. Stuffed portions, machine appliquéd, hand embellished, machine quilted. The inspiration for animals and nature is credited to Ansel Adams and Lorel Eiseley.

Columbia Basin pygmy rabbit: Cotton fabric, tulle, organza, wool batting. Raw-edge machine appliquéd. The quilt was based on a photograph taken by retired wildlife biologist Jim Witham, and was used as inspiration with his enthusiastic permission. Jim told Etta that this rabbit happened to be exceptionally photogenic. Etta says it must have been having a "good hare day."

common spiny lobster: Cotton fabrics, batiks, tulle. Machine appliquéd, corals stuffed for dimension, free motion and decorative machine stitched, embellished.

conservancy fairy shrimp: Cotton fabric, acrylic paint. Sketched, painted, machine pieced and quilted.

Cook Inlet beluga whale: Cotton fabric, organza, tulle, fusible, and glue. Susan Carlson's appliquéd technique, layered, machine quilted.

corpse flower: Cotton fabric, fusible web, tulle. Raw-edge machine appliquéd and machine quilted.

Costa Rican puma: Cotton batik, cork fabric, Tsukineko® inks, Derwent® Inktense Pencils, Neocolor II pastels. Painted, machine appliquéd, and free-motion stitched for dimension. Acknowledgment to Leah Huyghe for the picture on Unsplash.com, which inspired this quilt.

Cuban crocodile: Cotton print and batik fabric, Pellon Fabric Magic, Pellon Wonder Under, wide variety of threads, DecoArt Triple Thick Gloss Glaze, puffy 3-D paint. Machine pieced, hand appliquéd, machine appliquéd, machine quilted, depth created with stuffed batting, painted. Janet says that five weeks after her husband's death, she was trying to redefine the "me" without the "we." She decided to define herself as a fiber artist, and the call for entries for this project was the impetus to get on that path. Janet used her own photos taken at the Smithsonian National Zoo. She says one of the crocodiles seemed to pose for her.

Cuban painted snail: Upholstery fabrics, hand-painted fabrics, Inktense pencils, textile medium, wool batting, fusible. Painted, reverse trapunto, thread painted, machine quilted. Debbie is inspired by Fibonacci; she fell in love with the vibrant beauty of *polymitas* when she first saw them at the Smithsonian Museum of Natural History.

dama gazelle: Cotton fabric, colored pencils, Micron pens, fabric ink. Sketched and painted, machine quilted. Photos in the public domain from the Frankfurt Zoo used as reference.

Davis' green pitaya: Cotton fabric, fusible fleece, hedgehog quills. Turned-edge and raw-edge machine appliquéd.

Devil's Hole pupfish: Cotton fabric, various threads, watercolor and acrylic paints. Fabric painted, machine pieced, machine quilted, hand stitched. Photos from the USFWS website were inspiration. As a child, Diane was fortunate to grow up across the street from a wildlife reservation. She spent hours in the woods, practicing catch and release with fish, crayfish, turtles, snakes, grasshoppers, crickets, salamanders, frogs, and toads. She and a friend knew the best places to find fossils, walking for miles in silence and enjoying the beauty and solace of nature. They kept whatever pets their families would allow.

Dixon's ground snake: Commercial cottons, tulle, snakeskin, various threads, oil paint, fabric markers. Fabric painted, machine pieced and quilted, hand stitched.

dwarf bearclaw poppy: Cotton print fabric, batik. Machine quilted, appliquéd. A photo courtesy of the Utah Native Plant Society was used for inspiration.

elegant sunbird: Stabilizer, batik fabrics, dyed and ombré cotton fabrics, silk, fabric paints, fusible, colored pencils, Neocolor II pastel crayons, various threads. Drawn, hand appliquéd, machine appliquéd, thread painted, embellished, painted, colored, machine quilted. Nancy learned techniques she used from online classes by Melinda Bula for iQuilt and from Bula's book *Cutting-Garden Quilts.*

elk: Commercial cotton batik, cork fabric, Tsukineko® inks, Derwent® Inktense Pencils. Painted, machine appliquéd, and free-motion quilted. Laura acknowledges her husband, Jeffrey, as the photographer for this quilt's inspiration. While on a trip to Yellowstone National Park, they spotted an elk calling for his herd. It was a magical moment that they witnessed and captured first in a photo, and now in fiber art.

Eskimo curlew: Commercial cottons. Machine appliquéd and free-motion stitched.

Euphorbia cap-saintemariensis: Cotton fabric, yarn, Lutradur, acrylic paint, beads. Drawn, painted, woven, bargello-style machine-pieced background, machine stitched. While visiting the US Botanic Garden in Washington, DC, Hollis photographed this interestingly shaped plant and used her picture as the inspiration for this project. She says she could just hear it whisper, "Oh, please pick me."

European eel: Cotton batik and prints, dupioni silk, satin, organza fabric and ribbon, various yarns and threads. Layered, collaged, raw-edge machine appliquéd, decorative stitched, free-motion quilted, couched, layered. Methods used were learned in several workshops by Susan Carlson, Katie Pasquini-Masopust, and Judy Gula at Artistic Artifacts.

Florida manatee: Hand-painted silk charmeuse, hand-dyed silk dupioni. Hand appliquéd, trapunto, hand quilted and *sashiko* stitched. Thanks to the US Geologic Service for posting a video on YouTube from which Ricki drew the manatee. She and her husband regularly vacation in the Florida Keys, where they have had the honor of meeting manatees face to face.

Florida panther: Cotton fabric. Raw-edge machine appliquéd, thread painted, free-motion quilted. Lois took a helpful online class through craftsy.com titled "Thread Painting Essentials: Photorealistic Quilts," taught by Pam Holland. Lois's new home state is Florida, and she proudly displays a "Protect the Panther" license plate on her car.

Galápagos land iguana: Cotton fabrics including batiks and hand dyes, vintage Japanese kimono silk, nylon tulle, and a variety of threads. To come up with her design, Susan used some "low-tech" tools: a Tracer projector, gridded patternmaking paper, painter's tape, a step ladder, and a makeshift darkroom in her laundry room to enlarge a photo to make a pattern. Once she had a pattern, she traced individual pattern pieces and outlined the design on a muslin foundation. Fusible web was applied to each fabric before each piece was cut out. The pieces were placed on the muslin and fused in place. She credits her husband, Manny Fernandez, for the photo she used, taken on Santa Cruz Island, Galápagos, Ecuador. In October 2013, Susan, her husband, and her sister were part of a National Geographic expedition to the Galápagos. Their hike on Santa Cruz Island to Cerro Dragon (Dragon Hill) rewarded them with sightings of one of the many varieties of goldfinch endemic to the Galápagos, as well as three iguanas well off the trail; they saw more at the Darwin Research Center.

ghost orchid: Silk and cotton fabric. Raw-edge machine pieced block construction and raw-edge machine appliquéd. Terry learned about ghost orchids during her time in Florida as artist in residence at Everglades National Park.

giant clam: Cotton, lace, organza, ink. Layered, machine quilted, stuffed for more dimension, appliquéd. Neville Howarth took the photograph used for reference.

giant panda: Batik and woven cottons. Raw-edge appliquéd, machine pieced and quilted; this style of animal portraiture was taught by Maria Elkins. Image used is from Nicki's own photograph of Tai Shan, the giant panda that lived at the National Zoo in Washington, DC, from 2005 to 2010. This was the first panda cub born at the National Zoo that survived more than a few days. He was a celebrity in DC until he was called home in 2010 by his owner, the Chinese government. Tai Shan recently celebrated his 12th birthday at the China Conservation and Research Center for the Giant Panda.

ginkgo: Cotton fabric, Angelina®, angora yarn, beads. Whole cloth quilt; bleached, couched, hand embellished. Nancy thanks Kris Bishop for teaching fabric discharge techniques. Nancy wanted to make this quilt because ginkgo trees lined a street where she used to live, and she loved the sound their rustling leaves made.

giraffe: Cotton, cherrywood sueded and batik fabrics, Wendy Richardson Quilt Tapestry Studio landscape overdyes, suede fringe. Sketched, hand appliquéd, machine pieced, hand embroidered.

golden lion tamarin: Hand-dyed fabrics, fabric markers, paint sticks, stabilizer. Machine appliquéd, thread painted, machine quilted.

golden parakeet: Cotton fabric. Machine appliquéd, thread painted, quilted, and decorative stitched.

goldstreifiger: Cotton fabric. Sketched, machine appliquéd and quilted.

Grandidier's baobab tree: Cotton, silk, and linen fabric and a variety of threads. Machine stitched and appliquéd, hand appliquéd. Seed pod images of baobabs in the public domain used for reference. The tree depicted was inspired by a baobab tree image in Wikimedia Commons.

green peafowl: Hand-dyed and commercial fabrics, fusible web, oil pastels, soft pastels, and permanent markers. Painted, drawn, raw-edge machine appliquéd and quilted. This presentation was inspired by a photograph taken by Jeremy Holden, who gave his permission for use. Holden is a photographer and field biologist who works in association with Flora and Fauna International. Sherri says each art quilt class she takes and every technique she learns informs her design process. Few animals are as awe inspiring as the peafowl; their verdant hues are mesmerizing. This is her first effort to design an animal-inspired quilt.

hawksbill turtle: Commercial cottons, hand-dyed fabrics, crinkle tulle, organza, fabric paints, fabric-backed cork. Hand and machine appliquéd, painted, fabric manipulation, machine quilted. In August 2016, on a trip to Jamaica, Carole and her family were invited by Melvyn Tennant, the "Turtle Man" of the Oracabessa Bay Turtle Project, to witness the hatching of a nest of hawksbill turtles on a beach. It was amazing for them, grandchildren included, to watch and help 65 hatchlings bubble up from the sand, just before sunset, then begin their scramble to the sea. The females might survive and set their internal GPS to return to that same beach to lay their eggs in 20 years. Her quilt is titled *Hot Chicks, Cool Dudes: A Chance for Survival*; those were the words coined by Dr. Kimberley Stewart of the St. Kitts Sea Turtle Monitoring Network. The title refers to the fact that the sex of sea turtles is not determined at fertilization, but during incubation of the eggs in the nest. Warmer temperatures favor the development of females; cooler temperatures produce more males. She thanks Starla Phelps for introducing her to cork fabric.

Hector's dolphin: Commercial cottons and batiks, and a mesh onion bag. Machine appliquéd, longarm machine quilted. Teresa purchased permission to use a stock illustration from www.depositphotos.com to assist in color placement.

Hine's emerald dragonfly: Cotton fabric, opalescent fabric, stabilizer, beads, net, cheesecloth. Hand embroidered, free-motion quilted, machine and hand appliquéd. Carol Freeman (www.carolfreemanphotography.com) allowed use of her dragonfly photo for inspiration.

hippopotamus: Cotton fabric, Inktense blocks, yarn. Machine pieced, hand appliquéd, machine quilted. Vicente Lai, a personal friend of Rosanne's, took a photo while on safari in Serengeti National Park and granted permission for her to use it for inspiration.

Honduran emerald: Cotton fabric, various threads, acrylic paint mixed with textile medium, Fabrico markers, Lumiere paint, feathers. Low-emersion fabric dyed and painted, drawn, embroidered with artist-dyed yarns, shaded with markers and highlighted with paint, embroidered, free-motion thread painted, raw-edge appliquéd, trapunto. Inspiration came from a photo by Greg Homel.

Hong Kong camellia: Commercial cottons and batiks. Machine pieced, machine appliquéd. Donna thanks Terry Kramzar, who taught her to quilt individual squares, then sew them together to create a background, and then add an original appliquéd design on top.

honohono: Quilting fabrics, hand-dyed fabric, paint, organza. Drawn, machine pieced and appliquéd, thread painted, and machine quilted. Credit given to Serena Brown, who hand-dyed the green leaf fabric.

Indiana bat: Commercially printed fabric, beads, sequins, Texture Magic®. Machine pieced and appliquéd.

jaguar: Hand-dyed fabric, printed cottons, various threads, fabric marker, fabric paint. Layered, machine appliquéd, machine quilted.

jellyfish tree: Cotton batik fabric, various threads, fusible, Czech glass beads. Free-form raw-edge collaged, hand-pieced, machine appliquéd and quilted, hand embellished. In the summer Brenda often sits on a pier and watches umbrellas of jellyfish slowly pulse by, trailing tentacles behind. Intrigued to find this same form in nature as the fruit of a tree, she created a silent, lonely explosion of jellyfish in fiber art. This is her first art quilt; she thanks her mentor, Debbie Dempsey.

Juan Fernández firecrown: Cotton, hand-dyed and batik fabrics, various threads. Drawn, fabric collaged, machine quilted. Thank you to Professor Peter Hodum for a photo used as inspiration, with his permission. The techniques were learned in a class by Susan Carlson and by reading her books, Serendipity Quilts and Freestyle Quilts.

kakapo: Cotton fabrics, fusible web. Machine appliquéd and machine quilted. Karen and Jason say Douglas Adams, one of their favorite authors, came to their college and talked about his book Last Chance to See. One of the endangered animals he sought out was the kakapo; ever since, the kakapo has been a favorite of theirs. Thanks to Nancy Adams for making the fern frond.

Karner blue butterfly: Cotton fabric and yarn. Machine appliquéd, machine quilted, hand appliquéd.

Kaua'i white hibiscus: Cotton fabric, acrylic fabric paint. Raw-edge appliquéd, thread painted, fabric painted, machine stitched.

killer whale: Cotton fabric, a fusible product, fabric paint, Derwent® Inktense Blocks. Dyed fabric, raw-edge machine appliquéd, painted. Anna used a photo by Eli Martinez (www.sdmdiving.com) with permission for inspiration.

Kirtland's warbler: Cotton fabric, fabric paint. Raw-edge machine appliquéd, painted to add dimension. Anna credits the photo she used for inspiration to Emily Tornga.

komodo dragon: Cotton and synthetic fabric, artificial leather, cording, Swarovski® crystal, Pellon fleece. Appliquéd, machine embroidered. In 2015, Joanne went to Indonesia for five weeks, spending a day at the Komodo Island preserve. She was impressed with this threatening creature and, for this project, used her own photo as inspiration.

Lake Titicaca water frog: Cotton fabric, silk ribbons, tulle. Appliquéd, colored, and painted for accents and shading; couched, layered, machine quilted. A photo by Pete Oxford (www.peteoxford.com), a conservation photographer currently based in Ecuador, was used for inspiration, with his permission. Bobbie read an article online describing an occurrence in October 2016 where 10,000 Lake Titicaca frogs died. According to this National Geographic story, pollution was believed to be the cause of the deaths. Bobbie said reading of their plight made her heart ache.

lesser chameleon: Hand-dyed and commercial cotton fabric. Machine pieced and quilted, machine and hand appliquéd, as taught in a class by Terry Kramzar. Special thanks to Professor Christopher V. Anderson (www.chamaeleonidae.com), a biologist from the University of South Dakota, who gave permission to use a photo of a chameleon for inspiration.

loggerhead turtle: Batik and hand-dyed fabrics, stabilizer, tulle, wool roving, yarn, Dye-Na-Flow® dye, Tsukineko® Fabrico markers, various threads. Hand and machine appliquéd, free-motion quilted, painted, drawn, layered. Credit to John Barden of Blacksburg, Virginia, who took the photo used for reference and inspiration. Karin watched loggerhead turtles hatch on Fripp Island, South Carolina, and learned a lot from the dedicated volunteers who man the daily loggerhead patrol and help little hatchlings on their march to the ocean. Swimming above an adult turtle in the clear, blue waters off the Turkish coast deepened Karin's wish to make a sea turtle quilt.

long-billed tailorbird: Cotton and batik fabrics, angora yarn. Thread painted, machine appliquéd, hand and machine embroidered. Many years ago Sue took a thread-painting class from Libby Lehman. After some practice, she used this method to depict feathers on birds. Sue adds that seeing a video of the common tailorbird on Facebook touched her heart and soul. When building its nest, the female pierces the edges of leaves with her long bill. She then pulls plant fiber or spider silk through the holes, sewing the edges of the leaves together, which makes a cradle in which to build her nest.

longleaf pine: Cotton fabrics include hand dyed and hand painted. Machine pieced, various methods of appliqué, machine stitched. In her depiction, Eileen was drawn to the life cycle and how this tree has adapted to fires. The plant looks like a bush instead of a pine seedling, and it interrelates with other plants and animals in key ways in its habitat. The broken branch and acorn at the bottom of the quilt are half life-size.

Lord Howe Island stick insect: Commercial cottons and batiks. Machine quilted, machine appliquéd, free-motion and embroidery stitched. Teresa depicted the insects on her quilt in a representational style, with an aboriginal feeling.

Malayan tapir: Cotton, velveteen, Jacquard™ fabric paint, acrylic paint, textile medium, fusible web, various threads, markers. Shibori stitched, hand-painted fabric, machine stitched, machine quilted.

mandrill: Batiks, tulle, cotton fabric, heavy stabilizer, colored pencils, and fabric paint. Collaged and raw-edge machine appliquéd, embroidered, painted. Thanks to Carolyn Fulmer and Bonnie Anderson for offering advice and for sharing fabric for this project. This is Eileen's very first "challenge" quilt. Anano Miminoshvili granted permission to use her illustration.

maned wolf: Batiks and cottons. Hand appliquéd and hand quilted. A "floating block" was used to accent the wolves. Once she designed and drew all the blocks for this quilt, Karen used a photo by Oliver Feiler (https://photos.kiza.eu) for inspiration, with his permission.

markhor: Hand-felted wool and alpaca fibers, cotton fabric, beads. Hand felted, hand appliquéd, machine quilted, beaded, embroidered. Pam obtained permission by paying a fee to use an image for her inspiration from Shutterstock (www.shutterstock.com).

Menzies' wallflower: Hand-dyed and commercial cottons, various threads, Derwent® Inktense Blocks, Pigma pens. Machine pieced, raw-edge appliquéd, machine quilted.

Minnesota dwarf trout lily: Cotton fabric, crayons. Machine strip pieced, hand appliquéd. A photo by Phil Delphey of the Minneapolis Field Office, Region 5, USFWS, was used for inspiration. Dottie learned that no two leaves are alike on this lily; much like snowflakes, they all are different. As a child, she played in the woods on the edge of the Adirondacks in New York State, discovering plants and critters as she turned over logs and rocks.

Mitchell's satyr butterfly: Cotton fabric, tulle. Collaged construction as taught by Susan Carlson, raw-edge machine appliquéd. A photo by C. E. Bach and B. J. Barton provided inspiration and was used with permission.

Morefield's leather flower: Hand-dyed and commercial cotton, silks, lace, velvet, a variety of threads, netting. Strip-pieced background, layered, machine quilted and appliquéd. With permission, Dena used a photo by Todd Crabtree of the USFWS as a model for this piece. She enjoys macrophotography and created a macro version of this 4-inch flowering vine.

mountain sweet pitcher plant: Hand-dyed and commercial cotton fabric, colored pencils, inks, variety of threads. Machine pieced, appliquéd, quilted, drawn.

mountain yellow-legged frog: Cotton fabric, netting. Fabric collaged and free-motion machine quilted. Laura used photos from the Mountain Yellow-Legged Frog website for inspiration, with permission from Dr. Roland Knapp. As both a biologist and a fiber artist, Laura's quilt shows a story where people's actions can have unintended consequences; stocking normally fishless lakes in the Sierra Nevada with trout has led to the decline of this frog.

mountain zebra: Commercial cottons. Raw-edge appliquéd. Maggie found working with the stark palette of the zebra to be cool and refreshing. While other zebra quilts feature zebra heads in profile, hers projects a different image. Inspiration came from an image on Shutterstock, Inc., which she paid for to use.

Nellie cory dwarf cactus: Batik and cotton printed fabric, dupioni silk, satin, various threads, beads. Layered background, raw-edge appliquéd, free-motion quilted, hand embroidered, hand embellished. In researching this species, Suzanne studied online and at the local library and visited garden shops. She read, looked at hundreds of photographs and drawings in books and online, and went to her local Home Depot to look at cactus plants. These things all helped her come up with her original design. Using an actual cactus was most helpful, since she could see the textures and depth that no photograph had captured. She learned various methods to make this quilt from teachers Susan Carlson, Katie Pasquini-Masopust, and Judy Gula.

northeastern bulrush: Cotton fabric, printed and hand-dyed batik, watercolor paint, watercolor pencils, ribbon, felt. Painted, machine appliquéd, hand and machine sewn and embellished, free-motion quilted. This quilt was inspired by a photo taken by Susi vonOettingen, an endangered-species biologist with the New England Field Office of the USFWS in Concord, New Hampshire, with permission. Barbara says biologists call this plant a relict: a species that somehow survives in isolated areas, even though initially believed extinct.

northern brown kiwi: Batik and woven cotton. Raw-edge machine appliquéd in the style of teacher Esterita Austin, machine pieced and quilted. Photo credit for reference goes to Willowbank Wildlife Reserve in Christchurch, New Zealand. Nicki said creating a kiwi was a perfect opportunity to play with color. Although the brown kiwi is brown, she decided to make hers in kiwi green. She chose purple for the background for contrast.

northern hairy-nosed wombat: Cotton fabric, Tsukineko® inks, Derwent® Inktense Pencils, NeoColor II pastels, Shrink Magic. Painted and machine quilted. Consent was granted by ©The State of Queensland (Department of Environment and Science) to use an image on their website.

northern spotted owl: Batik and woven cottons. A pattern was made by using a photo by Kameron Perensovich, with permission. Raw-edge appliquéd, machine pieced and quilted.

northern white rhinoceros: Materials include cotton fabric, wool yarn, metal and gemstone beads, metal charms, old clock faces and gears, oil paint sticks, acrylic paint, and resin. Traditional nine-patch blocks, paper-pieced, raw-edge appliquéd and free-motion quilted, all combined to achieve a "steampunk" style. Karla uses found objects and developed a process for using resin to make animals on cloth.

ocelot: Commercial cottons. Raw-edge machine appliquéd, free-motion quilted. The inspiration for this quilt is an Aztec legend called "Las Manchas del Ocelote" (the ocelot's spots). As the story goes, many years ago, when the earth was paradise and all creatures lived in harmony, an ocelot lived on top of a hill, and its skin was like the sun: golden, shiny, and soft, without a single black spot. This majestic creature was a dreamer who loved the beauty of nature and his own beauty as well. Every night he spent hours admiring the sky, the moon, and the planets. One night he noticed a shooting star and became very envious. After many envious nights, watching the shooting star and yelling at it, the star responded that to see a shooting star is a privilege to be respected. The ocelot refused to see it this way, and the angry shooting star retaliated against the ocelot, shooting fire at it, covering the animal in black spots.

Ohlone tiger beetle: Cotton and wool fabric, various threads. Appliquéd and machine pieced. As the spouse of a career US Fish & Wildlife Service employee, concerns about the environment have always been a part of life in Linda's family. Before he retired, her husband worked with the Environmental Contaminants / Water Quality Division, in which insects play a major role.

Oregon spotted frog: Cotton fabric, fabric paint, watercolor pencils, markers, inks, lace, pewter charms. Appliquéd, colored, painted, embellished, machine quilted. Bobbie obtained information from her niece, Lisa, who is a manager for the USFWS at the Conboy Lake National Reserve. Lisa is at the forefront of trying to protect this species of frog. The photo used

for inspiration is courtesy of the Woodland Park Zoo in Seattle, Washington, with permission of the photographer, Ryan Hawk (www.RyanHawk.com).

ornate eagle ray: Commercial batiks, other cottons, and pearls. Machine appliquéd.

oyster mussel: Cotton, silk, and sheer fabrics. Drawn, used a thermofax screen made by Susan Price of PGFiber2Art to print the background, machine quilted, layered, embellished. Thanks to Joel Satore for permission to use his photo as reference, and to Dr. Amy Fowler, professor at George Mason University, for scientific advice.

Pacific pocket mouse: Cotton and silk fabric, recycled blue jeans, Inktense pencils, and acrylic paint. Closely studying US government photos from the US Geological Survey to better understand pocket mice, Lisa made small, actual-sized mice running in and out of blue-jean pockets. She researched articles about how to draw mice and sketched her own, painted them, drew their faces, and stitched on their whiskers. Pocket mice have distinguishing features, which she included: hair on the bottoms of their feet, slight light-colored patches near the base of their ears, and fur-lined cheek pouches in which they carry food. Machine and hand appliquéd.

Paiute cutthroat trout: Sheer synthetic and cotton fabric, various threads and embroidery floss, beads, polished stones, fabric paint. Machine appliquéd, thread painted and decorative stitched, layered, hand embroidered and beaded, painted.

pendant kihi fern: Cotton fabric, yarn and various other fibers, Inktense blocks. Hand and machine appliquéd, embroidered, hand and machine embellished, hand quilted. Inspired by a photo by a Seattle, Washington, NOAA scientist, Eric White, and used with permission.

Philippine eagle: Batik and cotton fabric, Derwent® Watercolor Pencils, Tsukineko® paints, fusible web. Pieced and machine appliquéd, collaged, painted, thread painted, machine quilted. Permission obtained from Evgen Silin of SuperColoring Art (www.super-coloring.com) to create the design from one of their images.

pink fairy armadillo: Cotton batik, synthetic fur, tulle, silk strips, various yarns, assorted threads. Fusible machine appliquéd on a whole-cloth background, hand embroidered, thermofax screen printed, machine quilted. In researching this tiny animal she had never heard of, Susan heard of a specimen at the Smithsonian Natural History Museum, so she went there and took pictures, which were the basis for this quilt.

pink waxcap: Cotton fabric. Regina modifies an image with round or smooth design outlines until she achieves a drawing consisting of only straight lines. This drawing is further dissected into individual segments and serves as a base for intricate paper piecing. After sewing all the individual segments, she reassembled all the parts to display the entire picture. Free-motion machine quilting connects all layers of the quilt, front, inner batting, and back and emphasizes the surface structure of the mushrooms. She obtained permission to use a photo by Dr. Wolfgang Prüfert of Germany for the basis of this quilt. Regina says nature connects her as a human being with the great cycle of life. In addition to the joy of nature, she feels great concern. The global changes are reducing the habitats of many species; this affects even inconspicuous mushrooms. Fungi are omnipresent in medicine and exist as beneficial or harmful molds in our meals. In forests and meadows they have immense ecological significance. They interact with soil organisms and plants and ensure the recycling of organic matter. There is still much to explore in science, but one thing is sure: a world without elephants would be changed and sad, but in a world without mushrooms, the cycle of life would come to a standstill.

piping plover: Assorted fabrics. Machine pieced, raw-edge appliquéd, free-motion quilted. Laura means for this quilt to read like a comic book, titled "Going, Going, Gone." The story shows the disappearance of a species and the hole that will be left if the species becomes extinct.

Pismo clarkia: Commercial cotton fabric, ecoprinted linen, fabric paint, fusible web. Fusible appliquéd, painted, thread painted, machine quilted. Credit is given to Tanya Prather for the ecoprinting fabric used as part of the background. Ellen wanted her quilt to showcase the precious detail found in each blossom. She hopes that focusing on this easily overlooked species might inspire conservation efforts to help tiny but still unique life forms.

polar bear: Cotton batiks and hand dyes, cotton prints, fusible web. This quilt began with a photo of a polar bear that Luana took in Churchill in Manitoba, Canada, on the edge of the Arctic Circle. In Photoshop she added the image of the solar eclipse in the sky. She drew this onto white muslin and worked on a light box to cut out pieces of fabric, using fusible backing, to create a jigsaw collage of the image. Once the collage was completed, she thread painted, added the batting and backing, and then added more machine quilting to create the final design. She says the polar bears can feed only when the ice is frozen. Now that the ice is melting one month early, and freezing one month later, they have lost two crucial months of feeding time per year. As a mother, artist, business owner, and citizen of the world, she uses her art as her voice to educate and, she hopes, inspire others to take action.

popolo ku mai: Cotton, silk, faux leather, faux suede, beads. Free-form cut, raw-edge machine appliquéd and quilted, 3-D construction, and painted.

proboscis monkey: Cotton fabric, flannel, canvas, watercolor paint, yarn. Painted, fringe made by separating cotton weaving, raw-edge machine appliquéd.

Przewalski's horse: Leather, Derwent® Watercolor Pencils, batik fabric. Kim used a Smithsonian Zoo picture for inspiration, drew a simplified version, and stitched leather on a HandiQuilter midarm sewing machine and on a Bernina machine. She added details with watercolor pencils.

Puerto Rican amazon: Cotton and polyester fabric, yarn, ink. Hand and machine appliquéd, machine pieced and quilted, machine embroidered.

purple-faced langur: Cotton and hand-dyed fabrics, colored pencil and ink. Various methods of appliqué and collage, machine stitched, drawn, and colored for detail. Eileen says giving each individual langur personality and action was her challenge. In order to show the habitat loss in Sri Lanka, she researched the cityscape of Colombo, the financial center of the country, and included some iconic structures.

pygmy three-toed sloth: Commercially printed fabric, Texture Magic®, beads, and sequins. Machine appliquéd and pieced, hand embellished.

quokka: Commercial cotton, including aboriginal fabric. Strip-pieced background, raw-edge appliquéd, machine quilted. Permission was granted to use an image for inspiration by Rottnest Fast Ferries: www.rottnestfastferries.com.au.

rainbow leaf beetle: Hand-painted and commercial cotton fabrics, drapery liner, airbrush ink, aloe, satin varnish. Machine appliquéd, quilted. Thanks to research entomologists Drs. David Furth and Alexander Konstatinov for showing Linda the collections of rainbow leaf beetles at the Smithsonian Museum of Natural History when she was researching her quilt. As a former biologist, she enjoyed a behind-the-scenes look. When she searched the internet for images, she loved looking at the water-bubble-covered photos that she found.

rainbow parrotfish: Organza, cotton fabric, fusible web, various threads. Layered, machine and hand stitched. Dabney says Puerto Rico was devastated by hurricanes in 2017. There was a toll on human lives, and on animal lives. How many species that were already at risk became more endangered because of the hurricanes? She wants to honor all the creatures of Puerto Rico with this quilt.

red panda: Cotton fabric, fabric paint, various threads, fusible web. Machine stitched, painted, stuffed for dimension, machine appliquéd, and thread painted.

red-cockaded woodpecker: Cotton, beads, fabric markers, metallic threads, paint, and pencils. Raw-edge appliquéd, machine quilted, hand embroidered, penciled and painted details. Pat began her quilt by taking photographs in a park near her home both of the environment and the birds. She opened her photos in an editing program and made a composition. She prepared paper to the quilt size and drew an image. She traced parts of the drawing and transferred this to fabric; putting the quilt together is like assembling a jigsaw puzzle.

red-crowned crane: Cotton and batik fabrics, various threads, beads. Machine appliquéd, machine quilted, *sashiko* hand stitched, beaded. This design was derived from a pattern design by Mochi Mochi Fiber Art, with permission. While living in Okinawa, Japan, Ann watched these birds as they closely followed farmers in rice paddies. Small fish, driven from their hiding places among rice reeds, were snatched up and eaten by the cranes. The scene was captivating. The slow, peaceful, and methodical pace of the fieldworkers was counterbalanced by the beauty and grace of the cranes, watching like sentinels. As depicted on this quilt, the relationship between the island people and nature is reverent and instills the belief that we can exist in harmony.

reindeer: Cotton cloth, handmade and machine-made lace doilies. Appliquéd with overlay of lace, machine and hand stitched. Tamara thanks her husband, Roger Webb, who drew the reindeer design.

ring-tailed lemur: Knee socks, cotton fabric, fleece, pleather. Hand appliquéd, machine quilted. Thanks to Joseph Sovey for the quilt design.

rock gnome lichen: Kathy and Nancy worked together with cotton, linen, denim, and various yarns and threads to use crazy-quilt piecing and appliqué techniques. They chose to depict this species because they could not resist something with the word "gnome" in the title.

Rugel's pawpaw: Cotton fabric, fusible web, various threads. Raw-edge machine appliquéd and quilted. Lynn was inspired by Paul Rebmann's Wild Florida Photo Nature Photography website: www.wildflphoto.com. He granted permission to use his photo of the pawpaw to reproduce with fabric in an abstract manner.

rusty patched bumble bee: Kris learned how to hand-dye her own fabric for this quilt in a class by Pauline Davy; other materials include velvet, polyester fur, painted cheesecloth, and various yarns. Machine appliquéd, machine quilted, embellished.

Ruthvens kingsnake: Cotton and polyester fabric, various threads, piping cord. Collaged, raw-edge machine appliquéd, layered, extra stuffing for dimension, machine and hand stitched, hand embellished.

San Joaquin kit fox: Cotton fabric. Drawn, machine pieced and appliquéd, thread painted. Crystal is a self-taught quilter who has not taken any classes.

sandplain gerardia: Cotton fabric, embroidery thread. Hand appliquéd and embroidered. Anne Nelson cross-stitched the bumblebee. Dottie depicted this plant because it was one of the first from her home state of New York to be considered endangered. She has been an environmentalist beginning in college, 60 years ago.

scalloped hammerhead shark: Commercial and hand-dyed cotton fabric, various threads, beads, foil overlay. Drawn, machine pieced and appliquéd, machine quilted, hand beaded, foiled.

Shenandoah salamander: Hand-dyed cottons, paint, markers, fusible, poly/nylon. Machine appliquéd, colored, painted, machine quilted. Jane took a class by Carol Shinn that inspired thread painting.

short-tailed chinchilla: Hand-dyed and commercial cotton fabric, wool, buttons. Raw-edge appliquéd, needle-felted, machine quilted.

Silverstone's poison frog: Cotton fabric, organza, beads, various threads, fabric pencils. Raw-edge appliquéd, drawn. Pat began research for this quilt by visiting the Baltimore Aquarium and photographing the poison frogs she saw there to use as reference. The organza, when topped with red metallic thread, made the frog sparkle. Thread painting gave the leaves texture.

silversword: Fabrics painted by the artist, other painted fabrics, and commercial fabrics. Raw-edge appliquéd and machine quilted. On Kathleen's 50th birthday, she and her husband drove to the top of the Maui volcano Haleakala at dawn. It was cloud covered and cold. As the sun rose through the mist, they witnessed an unforgettable landscape. The crater was magnificent in scope, and within the large crater was a string of smaller craters that made Kathleen think they were on the moon. The only plants growing in the hard-scrabble of the extinct volcano were the silversword.

Singapore freshwater crab: Cotton batiks, hand-dyed and commercial quilting cotton, stabilizer, netting, various threads. Torn strips to form the background in an adapted version of a class taught by Lisa Ellis. Machine quilted, machine appliquéd. The photo used for inspiration was taken by Christophe Puan at https://frogtographysg.carbonmade.com.

slender chub: Fusible web, cotton fabric, Dertwent® Inktense blocks, Pigma Micron pens. Machine-pieced background, appliquéd, machine quilted. Thanks to Becky Heavner for help with the central focus, and to Carole Nicholas for advice on the use of shading.

slow loris: Batik fabric, fusible web. Raw-edge appliquéd, machine quilted, thread drawn and thread painted. In 2015 Meggan went to see the National Geographic Photo Ark exhibit at the National Geographic Museum in Washington, DC. This project was begun to create portraits of the world's species before they disappear, and to inspire people everywhere to care. Her personal response, as well as observed responses of others viewing the exhibit, was moving. She hopes that this project has the same effect to inspire and inform its viewers.

small whorled pogonia: Cotton quilt fabric, various threads, nylon tulle, fusible web, stabilizer, Micron pen, acrylic paint, yarn. Raw-edge collage appliquéd, machine stitched, couched, hand appliquéd.

smooth coneflower: Cotton quilting fabric, various threads, fabric paint, oil pastels. A curved improvisational machine-piecing method as taught by Cindy Grisdela was used. The flower petals were hand-appliquéd using the "Apliquick" method of Rosa Rojas. Bonnie made the central cone of the flower by using different sizes of pompoms and enhanced the entire design with fabric paint and oil pastels. Special thanks to Rob E. Evans, Natural Areas protection manager with the Virginia Department of Conservation and Recreation in Richmond, Virginia, for permission to use a photo as inspiration.

snow leopard: Commercially printed and hand-dyed fabrics, recycled fabric from clothing, nylon tulle, various threads. This quilt began with a trip to Toronto, where Ricki and James McCann photographed the cub at the Toronto Zoo. She used both of their photos as reference in making this piece. She thanks Christy MacMorran, who taught her to paint and spent two years helping her see the world through a painter's eyes.

South Island wren: Cotton, velvet and silk fabric, fabric paints and paint sticks. Traditional piecing methods, machine appliquéd, paint applied to add color, highlights, and texture. Gay learned that these birds are collectors of feathers, which they use in their nests. She turned the wren on this quilt into a true collector: he is shown admiring his exotic collection of feathers.

southern rockhopper penguin: Cotton, tulle, velvet, recycled clothing. Fabric collaged, machine pieced and quilted. Karen thanks Susan Carlson for teaching and guiding her in the process of making this quilt. Paul Selva gave permission to use his photo that inspired her quilt. Karen was first a traditional quilt maker. Her friend Ricki Selva said she could do more with her creativity than re-creating others' ideas. Karen thanks Ricki for pushing her creatively and for introducing her to this endangered species project. Karen was fortunate to travel to New Zealand, where she saw a rockhopper off the southern coast.

southern sea otter: Commercially printed fabrics, hand-dyed and recycled fabric, nylon tulle, various threads. Collaged, raw-edge appliquéd, machine quilted. This quilt began in a five-day workshop with Susan Carlson. Ricki thanks Christy MacMorran, her painting teacher. Thanks to Mike Baird of Morro Bay (http://bairdphotos.com), who took the photo that inspired this quilt. She thanks Karen Coan for traveling to Elkhorn Slough and Moss Landing to observe the resident sea otters firsthand.

Speke's gazelle: Cotton fabrics, fabric markers, paint, crayons. Machine stitched and quilted, drawn, colored, marked, and painted. Photo by Robert Shepardson used with permission for reference.

spruce-fir moss spider: Quilting cotton fabric, tulle, Inktense pencils, fusible. Layered, machine appliquéd, colored, machine quilted. Bonnie Hunter gave permission to use her "North Carolina Moss" pattern for the background. Gary Peeples of USFWS provided photos of the spider for reference; the focal point in this piece is a composite of several photos and illustrations.

staghorn coral: Hand-dyed cotton fabric. Hand appliquéd, machine quilted. Kathy saw an edition of *CBS Sunday Morning* that told about the bleaching occurring on the Great Barrier Reef. This piece interprets the footage she watched from that show, as the camera scanned miles and miles of dead coral.

Sumatran orangutan: Fabric, hand-dyed felted wool. Kerry used a felting machine to embed hand-dyed local wool for the fur on this quilt. She was eager to depict the orangutan; her godfather was the head vet at the Bronx Zoo, where Kerry regularly visited and fed baby primates.

Sunda pangolin: Cork, hand-dyed and batik fabrics, wool batting, fusible web, Shiva Oil Paintsticks. Machine appliquéd. The artists credit Andrew Saffron, art teacher at Lake Braddock Secondary School in Burke, Virginia, who drew the pangolin. They say these scaly yet charming critters are a study in geometric patterns, making them an interesting textile art composition. Creative mindsets brought together a quilting camaraderie, encouraging them to use their individual gifts to bring the fabric pangolin to life.

swamp pink: Commercial and hand-dyed and painted fabric, ink pencils, pastel dye sticks. Machine appliquéd, machine quilted. Bunnie says people usually think of animal life when they think of endangered species. She wanted to represent threatened plant life in our own backyard. This species is a Virginia native wildflower.

tansy beetle: Cotton and silk fabrics, beads, oil paint sticks, India ink, acrylic paints, fusible web. Raw-edge machine appliquéd and quilted, painted. Lisa believes that insects are underappreciated for their beauty, even though during Victorian times these beetles were thought so attractive that their wing cases were used for sequins.

Taylor's checkerspot butterfly: Quilting cotton, flannel, fusible web, encased welting, Lutradur®, seed beads and bugle beads, illusion, chenille stems, "fun" fur. Machine appliquéd, embellished, and quilted. The Lutradur® "burns" in circular and interesting shapes, so Tina says it is great for butterfly wings. She says the butterfly needed to fly; hence the 3-D wings. Then everything became 3-D: stems, leaves, eggs, caterpillars, chrysalis. Quilted by Terry Chase.

tiger: Cotton fabric, fusible web, colored pencils, Sharpie® markers. Hand embroidered, raw-edge appliquéd. Jeanie used a picture by Pexels.com for her inspiration; the image is in the public domain.

tundra swan: Hand-woven cotton, silk organza, Inktense watercolor pencils, stabilizer, poly mesh, feathers. Layered, appliquéd, colored, machine quilted.

ultramarine lorikeet: Cotton fabrics, various threads, fusible web, Tsukineko® inks. Collaged, machine appliquéd, and free-motion threadwork, with ink added for shading.

Vancouver Island marmot: Cotton fabric. Pictorial hand appliquéd, machine quilted. Design adapted from the artist's own photograph.

Virginia big-eared bat: Cotton fabric, fusible product, Derwent® Inktense Blocks. Raw-edge machine appliquéd, painted and drawn for dimension and detail.

Virginia sneezeweed: Cotton fabric, buttons, embroidery thread, and Karen's mom's handkerchief. Appliquéd, embroidered, hand-quilted, pieced border. Karen received permission from C&T Publishing to use their

books A Gathered Garden and Butterflies & Blooms, both by Carol Armstrong, for ideas to make the flowers.

West African ostrich: Cotton sateen and other fabric, paint. Free-motion quilted, hand-painted. Disney's balletic ostriches in the "Dance of the Hours" sequence in the movie Fantasia delighted Holly as a child and continue to do so. She is saddened by the thought that a child in the future might never know the majesty and hilarity of these animals. She sought to create a sense of delight and a palpable sense that they are disappearing.

western lowland gorilla: Batik and hand-dyed fabrics, fusible web, various threads. Drawn, layered, machine appliquéd.

western prairie fringed orchid: Cotton prints and batik fabric, stabilizer, various threads, Inktense ink blocks. Raw-edge machine appliquéd, free-motion quilted, shaded, thread painted. Suzanne thanks Peter M. Dziuk of Minnesota Wildflowers (www.minnesotawildflowers.info) and J. Fowler Photography (www.jfowlerphotography.com) for permission to use their photos for inspiration. She credits instructors Melinda Bula, Susan Carlson, Judy Gula, and Katie Pasquini-Masopust for lessons on design and construction.

western Santa Cruz giant tortoise: Batik and vinyl fabric, Ultrasuede®, paint, various threads. Collaged, painted, machine stitched, and thread painted on an Innova longarm sewing machine, trapunto. Kathy Adams Clark, a naturalist and photography teacher (www.kathyadamsclark.com), granted permission to use her photos. Starla says a joy of making art quilts is doing the research. She now has a sincere appreciation for these fascinating creatures of the Galápagos who survived for centuries in their isolated location until the advent of human intervention.

western snowy plover: Batik fabric, various threads, fusible web. Machine appliquéd.

whale shark: Cotton fabrics, various threads, paint. Drawn, painted, machine appliquéd, and machine quilted. Thanks to Steve Eilenberg and Marie Tartar of Aperture Arts (www.aperturephotoarts.com) for permission to use their photo for inspiration. While diving, Linda has seen a whale shark; she says it was a rare moment she will never forget.

white-bellied heron: Cotton thread, fabric, fusible web. Thread painted, free-motion quilted, machine appliquéd, stitched and quilted.

whooping crane: Cotton fabric, fusible web, colored pencils, Sharpie® markers. Paper pieced, string pieced, raw-edge appliquéd. Jeanie purchased permission from

Adobe Stock photos for inspiration for this quilt and credits Kellington / Adobe Stock©.

wild water buffalo: Cotton and cotton-blend fabric, synthetic sheers, Ultrasuede®, fabric paint. Machine appliquéd, quilted, embroidered, and painted. Joanne has seen similar impressive feral water buffalo in Australia, where they are not native. She used her own photos as inspiration.

woodchat shrike: Hand-dyed fabric, felted wool, Ultrasuede®, silk and cotton threads, seed beads, and a vintage glass button. Machine appliquéd and quilted, hand appliquéd, embroidered.

yellow teardrop butterflyfish: Cotton fabric, Inktense pencils, tulle, fusible web. Drawn, layered, machine appliquéd, free-motion quilted.

Special Thanks to Our Sponsor:

BIBLIOGRAPHY

Active Wild: Wildlife & Science News. www.activewild.com. Accessed July 4, 2018.

Africa Geographic. https://africageographic.com.

African Wildlife Foundation. https://www.awf.org.

"*Agilinis acuta*." Go Botany: New England Wild Flower Society. https://gobotany.newenglandwild.org/species/agalinis/acuta/. Accessed July 4, 2018.

Alaska Fisheries Science Center. www.afsc.noaa.gov.

Alderfer, Jonathan. *National Geographic Backyard Guide to the Birds of North America*. Washington, DC: National Geographic, 2011.

All about Wildlife. www.allaboutwildlife.com.

American Midland Naturalist. www.bioone.org/loi/amid.

Animal Corner. https://animalcorner.co.uk/.

Animal Diversity Web. https://animaldiversity.org.

Animal Fact Guide. https://animalfactguide.com.

Animalia: All You Want to Know about Animals. http://animalia.bio.

Animals Network. http://animals.net.

Animals Time. http://animalstime.com.

AnimalSake. https://animalsake.com.

Atkinson, Rachel, Patricia Jaramillo, Walter Simbaña, Anne Guezou, and Vanesa Coronel. "Advances in the Conservation of Threatened Plant Species of Galapagos." *Galapagos Report*, 2007–2008. www.galapagos.org/wp-content/uploads/2012/04/biodiv1-threatened-plant-species.pdf. Accessed July 4, 2018.

"Attenborough's Long-Beaked Echidna (*Zaglossus attenboroughi*)." Web Animal and Nature Ambassadors. November 2, 2014. https://jaspertapen.wordpress.com/2014/11/02/attenboroughs-long-beaked-echidna-zaglossus-attenboroughi/. Accessed July 4, 2018.

A–Z Animals. https://a-z-animals.com.

BBC. www.bbc.com.

Benson, Sonia, and Rob Nagel. *Endangered Species*. 3 vols. Farmington Hills, MI: UXL, 2003.

Bird Endowment: Saving the Blues. www.birdendowment.org.

BirdLife International. www.birdlife.org.

Black-Footed Ferret Connections. http://blackfootedferret.org.

Buglife. www.buglife.org.uk.

Burton, Maurice, and Robert Burton. *International Wildlife Encyclopedia*. 22 vols. New York: Marshall Cavendish, 2002.

Cal Poly Pomona. www.cpp.edu.

California Department of Fish and Wildlife. www.wildlife.ca.gov.

The California Endangered Species Act. Fish & Game Code, §§ 2050 et seq.

California Native Plant Society. www.cnps.org.

California Native Plant Society, Rare Plant Program. Inventory of Rare and Endangered Plants of California (online edition, v8-03 0.39). www.rareplants.cnps.org. Accessed July 4, 2018.

The Cat House. www.cathouse-fcc.org.

Center for Biological Diversity. www.biologicaldiversity.org.

Center for Plant Conservation. https://saveplants.org.

Cheetah Conservation Fund. https://cheetah.org.

ChimpSaver.org. www.chimpsaver.org.

Convention on International Trade in Endangered Species of Wild Fauna and Flora (CITES). www.cites.org.

Cornell Lab of Ornithology. www.allaboutbirds.org.

Cornell Lab of Ornithology, Neotropical Birds. https://neotropical.birds.cornell.edu.

Cuba Explorer. https://cubaexplorer.com/cubaexplorer.com.

"Davis' Green Pitaya." Texas Parks & Wildlife Department. https://tpwd.texas.gov/huntwild/wild/wildlife_diversity/nongame/listed-species/plants/davis_green_pitaya.phtml. Accessed July 4, 2018.

Deatrick, Elizabeth. "Hope for the Honduran Emerald Hummingbird." *Audubon*, July 30, 2015. www.audubon.org/news/hope-honduran-emerald-hummingbird. Accessed July 4, 2018.

Defenders of Wildlife. https://defenders.org.

Dendrobates.org. www.dendrobates.org.

Department of Conservation, New Zealand. www.govt.nz/organisations/department-of-conservation.

Department of Environment and Science. www.des.qld.gov.au (formerly Department of Environment and Heritage Protection, www.ehp.qld.gov.au).

Department of Land and Natural Resources. http://dlnr.hawaii.gov.

Deutsche Gesellschaft für Medienwirkungsforschung e.V. www.dgmf-ev.de.

Duke Lemur Center. https://lemur.duke.edu.

Earth's Endangered Creatures. http://earthsendangered.com.

Edge of Existence Programme. www.edgeofexistence.org.

Elias, Thomas. *Complete Trees of North America: Field Guide and Natural History*. London: Chapman & Hall, 2000.

Encyclopedia Britannica. www.britannica.com.

Encyclopedia of Life. http://eol.org.

"Endangered and Threatened Wildlife and Plants: Proposed Endangered, Threatened, and Not Warranted Listing Determinations for Six Distinct Population Segments of Scalloped Hammerhead Sharks, Docket 111025652–3245–02, RIN 0648–XA798." Department of Commerce, National Oceanic and Atmospheric Administration. *Federal Register* 78, no. 66 (April 5, 2013): 20718.

Endangered Wolf Center. www.endangeredwolfcenter.org.

Environmental Conservation Online System, US Fish & Wildlife Service. https://ecos.fws.gov/ecp.

"*Erimystax cahni* (Hubbs & Crowe, 1956): Slender chub." FishBase. www.fishbase.de/summary/2780#. Accessed July 4, 2018.

Evolutionistx. https://evolutionistx.wordpress.com.

Fisheries Secretariat. www.fishsec.org.

Flora & Fauna International. www.fauna-flora.org.

Florida Fish and Wildlife Conservation Commission. http://myfwc.com.

Friends of the Wild Flower Garden. http://friendsofthewildflowergarden.org.

Galapagos Conservation Trust. https://galapagosconservation.org.uk.

Garden Guides. www.gardenguides.com.

Gardeningknowhow.com. www.gardeningknowhow.com.

"*Ginkgo biloba*." *Ginkgo biloba* the Endangered Plant, March 3, 2013. http://ginkgobilobatheendangeredplant.blogspot.com. Accessed July 4, 2018.

Giraffe Conservation Foundation. https://giraffeconservation.org.

"Giraffes Must Be Listed as Endangered, Conservationists Formally Tell US." *The Guardian*, April 19, 2017. www.theguardian.com/environment/2017/apr/19/giraffes-endangered-species-conservation-hunting. Accessed July 4, 2018.

Global Times. www.globaltimes.cn.

"Goldstreifiger: *Buprestis bplendens*." Endangered Species. https://goldstreifiger.weebly.com. Accessed July 4, 2018.

Green Global Travel. https://greenglobaltravel.com.

GRIT. www.grit.com/animals.

"GSLEP Forum, August 24, 2017, Session 2: Population Assessment of World's Snow Leopards." International Snow Leopard & Ecosystem Forum. www.globalsnowleopard.org/wp-content/uploads/2017/09/Snow-Leopard-Population-Assessment-August-24th-notes.pdf. Accessed July 4, 2018.

"A Guide to the Amphibians and Reptiles of California." www.californiaherps.com.

Handbook of the Birds of the World. www.hbw.com.

"Honduran Emerald." American Bird Conservancy. https://abcbirds.org/program/communities/Honduran-emerald. Accessed July 4, 2018.

Hutchins, Michael. *Grzimek's Animal Life Encyclopedia*. Vol. 10, *Birds*. 2nd ed. Detroit: Gale, 2002.

iNaturalist. www.inaturalist.org.

Indonesia-dhaka.org. www.indonesia-dhaka.org.

Instituto Nacional de Ecología y Cambio Climático. www2.inecc.gob.mx.

International Crane Foundation. www.savingcranes.org.

International Penguin Conservation Work Group. www.penguins.cl/about-penguins.htm.

International Snow Leopard & Ecosystem Forum. http://forum.globalsnowleopard.org.

International Takhi-Group. www.savethewildhorse.org/en.

Its Nature. www.itsnature.org.

IUCN 2017. The IUCN Red List of Threatened Species. Version 2017. www.iucnredlist.org.

IUCN Species Survival Commission, Cat Specialist Group. www.catsg.org.

IUCN Species Survival Commission, Polar Bear Specialist Group. http://pbsg.npolar.no/en.

"IVF Is Best Chance to Save Endangered Northern White Rhino, Scientists Say." *The Guardian*, January 28, 2015. www.theguardian.com/environment/2015/jan/28/ivf-best-chance-save-endangered-northern-white-rhino-scientists-say. Accessed July 4, 2018.

Jane Goodall Institute UK. www.janegoodall.org.uk.

"Juan Fernández Firecrown." Oikonos. http://oikonos.org/juan-fernandez-firecrown/. Accessed July 4, 2018.

"Juan Fernandez Firecrown *Sephanoides fernandensis*." Cornell Lab of Ornithology, Neotropical Birds. https://neotropical.birds.cornell.edu/Species-Account/nb/species/juffir1. Accessed July 4, 2018.

"Kakapo Recovery." Department of Conservation. www.doc.govt.nz. Accessed July 4, 2018.

"Komodo Dragon." SeaWorld Parks & Entertainment. https://seaworld.org/Animal-Info/Animal-Bytes/Reptiles/Komodo-Dragon. Accessed July 4, 2018.

Komodo Survival Project. http://komododragon.org.

La Paz Waterfall Gardens & the Peace Lodge. www.waterfallgardens.com/index.php.

Landscope America: The Conservation Guide to America's Natural Places. www.landscope.org.

Le Jardin Naturel. http://baobabs.com.

Lincoln Park Zoo. www.lpzoo.org.

Live Science. www.livescience.com.

Macdonald, David W., and Andrew J Loveridge, eds. *The Biology and Conservation of Wild Felids*. New York: Oxford University Press, 2010.

Mallorca Bird Watching. www.mallorcabirdwatching.com/birds.

"Marine and Anadromous Fish." National Oceanic and Atmospheric Administration, US Department of Commerce, National Marine Fisheries Service, June 29, 2017. www.nmfs.noaa.gov/pr/species/fish. Accessed July 4, 2018.

Marine Mammal Center. www.marinemammalcenter.org.

MarineBio. http://marinebio.org.

Maui Nō Ka 'Oi Magazine. https://mauimagazine.net.

McGrath, Anne, and Joanne Treffs. *Wildflowers of the Adirondacks*. Utica, NY: North Country Books, 1981.

Michael Cavendish Corporation. *Wildlife and Plants*. 13 vols. 3rd ed. New York: Marshall Cavendish Reference, 2007.

Michigan State University Extension, Michigan Natural Features Inventory. http://mnfi.anr.msu.edu.

Minnesota Department of Natural Resources. www.dnr.state.mn.us.

Minnesota Wildflowers. www.minnesotawildflowers.info.

Mongabay. www.mongabay.com.

Monkey Worlds. www.monkeyworlds.com.

Mountain Yellow-Legged Frog. http://mylfrog.info.

Mowbray, Sean. "Switzerland Pledges to Protect Nature, but Is It Enough?" *Culture Trip*, September 19, 2017. www.theculturetrip.com/europe/switzerland/articles/switzerland-pledges-to-protect-nature-is-it-enough. Accessed July 4, 2018.

National Aquarium. www.aqua.org.

National Audubon Society. *National Audubon Society Field Guide to North American Birds: Eastern Region*. 2nd ed. New York: Alfred A. Knopf, 1994.

National Geographic Kids. https://kids.nationalgeographic.com.

National Museums Liverpool (blog). http://blog.liverpoolmuseums.org.uk.

National Oceanic and Atmospheric Administration, US Department of Commerce. www.noaa.gov.

National Oceanic and Atmospheric Administration, US Department of Commerce, National Marine Fisheries Service. www.fisheries.noaa.gov. (formerly www.nmfs.noaa.gov)

National Park Service, Everglades National Park. www.nps.gov/ever.

National Wildlife Federation. www.nwf.org.

Nature Conservancy. www.nature.org.

NatureServe Explorer. http://explorer.natureserve.org.

New York State Department of Environmental Conservation. www.dec.ny.gov.

New Zealand Birds Online. http://nzbirdsonline.org.nz.

Ol Pejeta Conservancy. http://olpejetaconservancy.org.

Operation Migration. http://operationmigration.org.

Oregon Zoo. www.oregonzoo.org.

Otanewainuku Kiwi Trust. http://kiwitrust.org.

Otsego Community Connection. www.otsego.org.

Our Endangered World. www.ourendangeredworld.com.

Oxford Brookes University. www.brookes.ac.uk.

Pacelle, Wayne. "Chimps Deserve Better—and Things Are Getting Better for Them." Humane Society of the United States, September 14, 2015. https://blog.humanesociety.org/2015/09/chimps-deserve-better.html. Accessed July 4, 2018.

"Paiute Cutthroat Trout; *Oncorhynchus clarkii seleniris*." California Department of Fish and Wildlife, November 17, 2017. www.wildlife.ca.gov/Conservation/fishes/Paiute-Cutthroat-Trout. Accessed July 4, 2018.

Parks Canada. www.pc.gc.ca/en/index.

Perrine, Doug. *Sea Turtles of the World*. Stillwater, MN: Voyageur, 2003.

"Petition to List the Giraffe (*Giraffa camelopardalis*) under the Endangered Species Act." Center for Biological Diversity, Humane Society International, Humane Society of the United States, International Fund for Animal Welfare, and Natural Resources Defense Council, April 19, 2017. https://ecos.fws.gov/docs/petitions/92212/912.pdf. Accessed July 4, 2017.

Philippine Eagle Foundation. www.philippineeaglefoundation.org.

Pictures and Facts of Animals. http://thewebsiteofeverything.com.

"*Porpolomopsis calyptriformis*." WikiVisually. www.wikivisually.com/wiki/Porpolomopsis_calyptriformis. Accessed July 4, 2018.

"*Porpolomopsis calyptriformis* (Berk.) Bresinsky—Pink Waxcap." First Nature. www.first-nature.com/fungi/porpolomopsis-calyptriformis.php. Accessed July 4, 2018.

"Press Release from CNN—Nairobi, 20th November 2015." Ol Pejeta Conservancy. www.olpejetaconservancy.org/cnns-inside-africa-explores-rhino-conservation-in-kenya/. Accessed July 4, 2018.

Rafflesia. www.rafflesiaflower.com.

Rainforest Alliance. www.rainforest-alliance.org.

RelivEarth. http://relivearth.com/endangered-species.

The Reptile Database. http://reptile-database.reptarium.cz.

Ripple, Jeff. *Sea Turtles of the World*. Stillwater, MN: Voyageur, 1996.

Robbins, Chandler S., Bertel Bruun, and Herbert S. Zim. *Birds of North America: A Guide to Field Identification*. New York: St. Martin's, 2001.

Sakrison, David. *Chasing the Ghost Birds: Saving Swans and Cranes from Extinction*. Ripon, WI: Watson Street Press, 2007.

San Diego Zoo. http://zoo.sandiegozoo.org.

Santa Barbara Zoo. www.sbzoo.org.

Save the Rhino. www.savetherhino.org.

Sciencing.com. https://sciencing.com.

Scientific American (blog). https://blogs.scientificamerican.com.

Scientific American Magazine, web. www.scientificamerican.com.

seaotters.com. https://seaotters.com.

Seifert, Frank. "In Search of the World's Rarest Trout." Orvis News. https://news.orvis.com/fly-fishing/paiute-trout/. Accessed July 4, 2018.

"*Setonix brachyurus*—Quokka." Australian Government, Department of Environment and Energy, Species Threats Database. http://environment. gov.au/cgi-bin/sprat/public/publicspecies.pl?taxon_id=229. Accessed July 4, 2018.

"*Setonix brachyurus quokka*." University of Michigan Museum of Zoology, Animal Diversity Web. https://animaldiversity.org/accounts/Setonix_brachyurus. Accessed July 4, 2018.

Sibley, David. *The Sibley Guide to Birds*. New York: Alfred A. Knopf, 2008.

"Slow Loris—Facts and Info." *Animal Animal Animal* (blog). https://animal-animal-animal.blogspot.com/2013/10/slow-loris-facts-and-info.html. Accessed July 4, 2018.

Smithsonian's National Zoo & Conservation Biology Institute. https://nationalzoo.si.edu.

Snow Leopard Conservancy. http://snowleopardconservancy.org.

Snow Leopard Trust. www.snowleopard.org.

South Carolina Wildlife Federation. www.scwf.org.

"Southern Appalachian Creature Feature Podcasts." US Fish & Wildlife Service, Asheville Ecological Services Field Office. www.fws.gov/asheville/htmls/podcast_transcripts/barotrauma.html. Accessed July 4, 2018.

Spotts, Pete. "Saving West's Iconic Landscapes from Wildfires, One Steppe at a Time." *Christian Science Monitor*, July 2, 2015. www.questia.com/read/1P2-38471866/saving-west-s-iconic-landscapes-from-wildfires-one. Accessed July 4, 2018.

St. Louis Zoo. www.stlzoo.org/animals/abouttheanimals/reptiles.

Susanti, Indah. "Wildlife Wednesday: American Bison." Indahs: Dive, Travel & Photography. https://indahs.com/2018/06/20/american-bison/. Accessed July 4, 2018.

Sweet, Sam. Field Herp Forum. www.fieldherpforum.com.

Swinburne, Stephen R. *Sea Turtle Scientist*. Boston: HMH Books for Young Readers, 2015.

Swiss Ornithological Institute in Sempach. www.vogelwarte.ch/en/home.

Talbot, Sandra Looman, and Stephen S. Talbot. "A New Population of Aleutian Shield Fern (*Polystichum aleuticum* C. Christens.) on Adak Island, Alaska." *American Fern Journal* 92, no. 4 (October–December 2002): 288–293.

Tapir Specialist Group. http://tapirs.org.

Thai National Parks. www.thainationalparks.com.

ThoughtCo. www.thoughtco.com.

Tigers in Crises. www.tigersincrisis.com.

University of California at Davis, Genomic Variation Laboratory. http://gvl.ucdavis.edu.

University of Florida Institute of Food and Agricultural Sciences. https://ifas.ufl.edu.

University of Hawai'i. www.hawaii.edu.

University of Michigan Museum of Zoology. https://lsa.umich.edu/ummz.

University of Michigan Museum of Zoology, Animal Diversity Web. https://animaldiversity.org.

US Botanic Garden. www.usbg.gov.

US Botanic Garden Conservatory. www.aoc.gov/capitol-buildings/us-botanic-garden-conservatory.

US Department of Agriculture. www.usda.gov.

US Department of the Interior. www.doi.gov.

US Department of the Interior, Bureau of Land Management. www.blm.gov/oregon-washington.

US Fish & Wildlife Service, Conboy Lake National Wildlife Reserve. www.fws.gov/refuge/conboy_lake.

US Fish & Wildlife Service, US Department of the Interior. www.fws.gov.

US Forest Service, US Department of Agriculture. www.fs.fed.us.

US Geological Survey, US Department of the Interior. www.usgs.gov.

Utah Native Plant Society. www.unps.org.

Ventura Fish and Wildlife Office, US Fish & Wildlife Service. www.fws.gov/ventura.

"Virginia Natural Heritage Fact Sheet: Smooth Coneflower: *Echinacea laevigata*." Virginia Department of Conservation and Recreation. www.dcr.virginia.gov/natural-heritage/document/fselaevigata.pdf. Accessed July 4, 2018.

"Volunteer with Orangutans." The Great Projects. www.thegreatprojects.com/volunteer-with-orangutans. Accessed July 4, 2018.

Wagner, Warren L., Derrel R. Herbst, and S. H. Sohmer. *Manual of the Flowering Plants of Hawai'i*. Rev. ed. Honolulu: University of Hawai'i Press, 1999.

Washington Department of Fish & Wildlife. http://wdfw.wa.gov.

Wetlands International Flamingo Specialist Group. www.wetlands.org/our-network/specialist-groups/flamingo-specialist-group/.

White, Thomas, Jr., and Fernando Nuñez-Garcia. "From Cage to Rainforest." *Endangered Species Bulletin* 28, no. 4 (July–December 2003): 16.

Whooping Crane Eastern Partnership. www.bringbackthecranes.org.

Wild Cattle Conservation Project. www.wildcattleconservation.org.

Wildlife Conservation Society China. https://china.wcs.org/Wildlife.aspx.

"Wildlife Fact Sheets." Texas Parks & Wildlife Department. https://tpwd.texas.gov/huntwild/wild/species.

Wildlife Vets International. www.wildlifevetsinternational.org.

Wildscreen Arkive. www.wildscreen.org/arkive.

Wombat Foundation. www.wombatfoundation.com.au.

World Association of Zoos and Aquariums. www.waza.org/en/site/home.

World of Flowering Plants. https://worldoffloweringplants.com.

World Parrot Trust. www.parrots.org.

World Wide Fund For Nature. http://wwf.panda.org.

World Wildlife Fund. www.worldwildlife.org.

Xerces Society for Invertebrate Conservation. https://xerces.org.

Zoological Society London. www.zsl.org/conservation.

ARTIST INDEX

For information on contacting any of these artists about their fiber art,
email the author at dmdesotomailbox@gmail.com